Storage
1-2-3®

Meredith®
BOOKS

Storage 1-2-3®

Editor: Ken Sidey
Copy Chief: Terri Fredrickson
Publishing Operations Manager: Karen Schirm
Senior Editor, Asset and Information Manager: Phillip Morgan
Edit and Design Coordinator: Mary Lee Gavin
Editorial and Design Assistant: Renee E. McAtee
Book Production Managers: Pam Kvitne, Marjorie J. Schenkelberg,
    Rick von Holdt, Mark Weaver
Contributing Copy Editor: Don Gulbrandsen
Contributing Proofreaders: Janet Anderson, Brenna Eldeen,
    Sara Henderson, David Krause
Indexer: Don Glassman

Additional Editorial and Design contributions from
Abramowitz Creative Studios

Publishing Director/Designer: Tim Abramowitz
Graphic Designers: Kelly Bailey, Joel Wires
Photography: Image Studios
    Account Executive: Lisa Egan
    Photographers: Bill Rein, John von Dorn
    Assistants: Rob Resnick, Scott Verber
    Technical Advisor: Rick Nadke
Additional Photography: Doug Hetherington
Illustration: Jim Swanson, Performance Marketing

Meredith® **Books**

Executive Director, Editorial: Gregory H. Kayko
Executive Director, Design: Matt Strelecki
Managing Editor: Amy Tincher-Durik
Executive Editor/Group Manager: Benjamin W. Allen
Senior Associate Design Director: Tom Wegner
Marketing Product Manager: Brent Wiersma
National Marketing Manager—Home Depot: Suzy Johnson

Publisher and Editor in Chief: James D. Blume
Editorial Director: Linda Raglan Cunningham
Executive Director, Marketing: Steve Malone
Executive Director, New Business Development: Todd M. Davis
Director, Sales-Home Depot: Robb Morris
Executive Director, Sales: Ken Zagor
Director, Operations: George A. Susral
Director, Production: Douglas M. Johnston
Director, Marketing: Amy Nichols
Business Director: Jim Leonard

Vice President and General Manager: Douglas J. Guendel

Meredith Publishing Group
President: Jack Griffin
Senior Vice President: Bob Mate

Meredith Corporation
Chairman and Chief Executive Officer: William T. Kerr
President and Chief Operating Officer: Stephen M. Lacy

In Memoriam: E.T. Meredith III (1933-2003)

The Home Depot®

Marketing Manager: Tom Sattler
© Copyright 2006 by Homer TLC, Inc. First Edition.
All rights reserved. Printed in the United States of America.
Library of Congress Control Number: 2005929401
ISBN-13: 978-0-696-22290-0
ISBN-10: 0-696-22290-6
The Home Depot® and **1-2-3**® are registered trademarks of Homer
TLC, Inc.

Distributed by Meredith Corporation.
Meredith Corporation is not affiliated with The Home Depot®.

Note to the Reader: Due to differing conditions, tools, and individual skills, Meredith Corporation and The Home Depot® assume no responsibility for any damages, injuries suffered, or losses incurred as a result of following the information published in this book. Before beginning any project, review the instructions carefully, and if any doubts or questions remain, consult local experts or authorities. Because codes and regulations vary greatly, you always should check with authorities to ensure that your project complies with all applicable local codes and regulations. Always read and observe all of the safety precautions provided by any tool or equipment manufacturer, and follow all accepted safety procedures.

We are dedicated to providing accurate and helpful do-it-yourself information. We welcome your comments about improving this book and ideas for other books we might offer to home improvement enthusiasts. Contact us by any of these methods:
Leave a voice message at: 800/678-2093
Write to: Meredith Books, Home Depot Books
    1716 Locust St.
    Des Moines, IA 50309–3023
Send e-mail to: hi123@mdp.com.

How to use this book

You see the dream: You, your family, your house. Your home is the hub of activity, a stage for everyday life, passions, and pursuits. It's comfortable and inviting. There's a place for everything and the ambience is orderly. What's more—you find what you need or want in a flash.

Cut!

That's not exactly what it's like at your house? You're not alone. Far too many people spend far too much time—every day—looking for things. They spend way too much time putting things away and cleaning up.

That's where Home Depot Storage Solutions 1-2-3 comes in. It's full of information designed to help you get organized—and stay that way. Most of the ideas offered here will not be new to you. "Well, I knew that already," you might say. But do you do it all the time? Sometimes a friendly outside reminder will get you up and going. Especially when you can see the light at the end of the tunnel—right from the start.

(You might also find yourself saying, "That's a good idea. I never thought of that, I could...")

Put the right storage solutions in place and you'll spend less time picking up, putting away, and tracking down your stuff, and you'll have more time for life.

Whether your whole house needs a storage makeover, or you just need to fine-tune a pile, drawer, or closet, Home Depot Storage Solutions 1-2-3 is your guide to putting your stuff in its place—your way.

Room by room

This book tackles the problems room by room. But before you get to the rooms, you'll read about some of the basic ideas that are common to all storage problems—how to really decide whether to keep something, the basic principles of organization you need to use when you do get the clutter out of your life, the implements of storage, and countless ideas you can employ to increase your storage space without renovating your home (there are even a few of those ideas too).

The first spaces to tackle are entries and mudrooms, those transition spots for family members that seem to become home for countless objects (including clothing).

You will find bedrooms in Chapter 3, with plenty of attention paid to cleaning out the closets—the main repository (after the bed, perhaps) for things in disarray. You'll see why closet organizing systems have become so popular. They're adaptable, inexpensive, and you can get them up in a couple of days. No more sorting through the clothes looking for your shoes (or vice versa).

The family bathroom, in Chapter 4, comes next as the place of respite from the world. Not so in your house? Find help to get it back in shape. The same goes for the kitchen, Chapter 5, which is the main activity center in many homes. That makes it a major candidate for clutter, as you might have experienced yourself. Maybe one solution you'd find especially

valuable is getting a small desk off to the side for family "business." Or it may be as simple as hanging a pot rack above the stove so you can get to the pots and pans more easily.

Family rooms, home offices, hobby rooms, and utility areas all sprout special storage needs, which can't be solved in the same way you "fix" a problem in the bedroom. After all, would that row of metal cabinets really look good in the bedroom? (Actually they might. Just depends on your style.) Chapters 6 through 8 lay out detailed information about storage solutions that fit these rooms specifically.

Then in Chapter 9 comes the do-it-yourself part. It includes illustrations that show you how to assemble and install most of the major storage items on the market today. If you don't have any experience with these tasks, this chapter will function as a preview. If you've already put some of these units to work, treat the chapter as a refresher course. The chapter also includes plans and instructions for creating a couple of attractive features you can personalize for your home.

All in all, Home Depot Storage 1-2-3 can save you from hiring an organizational expert because this book will help make you the expert.

Storage 1-2-3®
Table of Contents

How to use this book 3

Chapter 1
STORAGE BASICS   6

Getting ready 8
Storage—It's personal 12
Making storage 14
Retrofit or renovate? 16
Systematize your spaces 20
The attractive factor 22
Getting the job done 23

Chapter 2
ENTRIES AND MUDROOMS   24

Entry strategies 26
Front entries and foyers 28
Back doors and mudrooms 30
Stashes for small stuff 32

Chapter 3
BEDROOMS   34

Coping with closets 36
Closet systems 38
Furniture 44
Children's rooms 46

Chapter 4
BATHROOMS   52

Storage layouts 54
Towels and linens 56
Toiletries and medicines 62
Staying organized 66
Functional display 67

Chapter 5
KITCHENS   68

Pots, pans, tools, and trays 70
Storing appliances 74
Dishes and glassware 76
Food storage 78
Shelves for showing off 82
Towels and cleaning supplies 86

Chapter 6
FAMILY ROOMS   90

Built-in storage 92   Entertainment centers 98
Freestanding units 96   On display. 101

Chapter 7
OFFICES AND HOBBY ROOMS   104

Matching office space to needs 106   Staying organized 114   The home workshop 122
Getting the most from your desk . . . 110   Hobby room storage 118

Chapter 8
UTILITY SPACES   124

Laundry rooms 126   Yard and garden tools 138   Outdoor sheds and bins 144
Making your (laundry) life easier . . . 130   Sports equipment and
Garage storage 134   household goods 140

Chapter 9
STORAGE PROJECTS   148

Fasteners and fastening 150   Installing clip-mounted wire systems . 160   Assembling plastic storage units 174
Level mounting every time 152   Installing melamine closet systems . . 162   Building a window storage seat 176
Assembly essentials 154   Adding pullout shelves 164   Constructing cubic storage units 182
Installing wall shelves 156   Freestanding cabinets and shelves . . . 170
Installing track-mounted
    wire systems 158

Resources 187
Index 188

Storage basics

One of the attributes that most of humankind apparently lacks is the ability to know how, when, and where to put the stuff they gather. Most are good at gathering (perhaps some leftover genetic trait), but few have the putting-it-back part perfected yet. This is a skill (a habit, actually), and it's one anyone can learn.

Storing things the right way does not accurately describe the process—because for all the prescriptions you'll hear for this malady, what matters is that you find a way of coping with your own mess. There are some principles that apply to all situations,

and that's what you'll find in this first chapter. Not rules as such, just guidelines along the path. You can get off the path if you want—maybe you've found a better way. That's good. This book will give you enough information to get you going. That is, after all, half the problem. Finding, building, buying, or making your own solutions can go quickly. It's the fun part. (Actually, sorting can be fun too.)

The real benefit of keeping things organized (apart from reducing stress) is that it gives you more time to do what you want in the places you want to do it in. It's not fun when an

Chapter 1 highlights

GETTING READY
Preparing for good storage is as important as finding good storage solutions.

8

STORAGE—IT'S PERSONAL
You don't need to follow anyone else's prescriptions for storage. Find your own style and do things your way.

12

MAKING STORAGE
Create your own storage solutions by combining some of the many designs and devices available.

14

RETROFIT OR RENOVATE?
Storage doesn't always require a makeover of the room. Employ any number of retrofit ideas to expand your storage space.

16

SYSTEMATIZE YOUR SPACES
A number of easy-to-install systems will simplify your storage needs.

20

THE ATTRACTIVE FACTOR
What's good to look at will tend to stay that way. Make storage solutions attractive.

22

GETTING THE JOB DONE
When you've learned all the principles, it's time to roll up your sleeves and get things done.

23

integral part of dinner prep is clearing away clutter to get to the pots and pans or when you have to gather a week's worth of newspapers to find your favorite movie chair.

Even if you're a pack rat at heart, but keep an apparently neat house by filling closets and spaces under the beds to hide decisions you've put off, there's hope for you. Here's a basic method that works for everyone: Get the stuff out of the room, sort it, throw it, or keep it, build for what's left, and put the stuff back. Good organization—that's all there is to it. You can see for yourself on the following pages. Really.

Getting ready

GOOD IDEA

HIRE A PRO

If you're thinking about hiring a professional organizer to whip your closets and storage systems into shape, you'll find them listed in the phone book and on the Internet.

Do you have a pile . . . a mass . . . a closetful of stuff? Do you remember when you'd look at your rooms and see neat shelves and uncluttered closets? Do those days seem like a long time ago? You want to slay this heap of stuff into orderly submission and store it efficiently—but where do you start? Well, read on—it's easier than you think. There's a method for removing this madness, and when you master the method, solving storage puzzles is a cinch.

Make a plan, "chunk it," and get started

The first thing to do is jot down the rooms you need to declutter. Don't leave out any area in your home. If you like, prioritize the list according to which rooms need help the most. Then list zones in each room: closet, dresser, vanity drawers. This creates manageable pieces, or chunks,

you can sort one at a time. When you've fixed one, cross it off the list. That feels good! Post the list, with cross-offs, where you can see it. If you're not one who gets inspired by lists, skip it and divide your messes mentally—tackle them one section at a time. You may even decide to throw the priorities out the window. The point is to get started.

Grab some sorting gear

Arm yourself with sorting gear. Here's what you'll need:

- Containers—see-through or opaque tubs, cardboard boxes, trash bags, or paper sacks.
- Tape—masking tape or duct tape, anything you can write on.
- Markers—washable or permanent, markers are the key to knowing at a glance where you put things.

Now you need to name your containers with tape. Here's how you should label them, and what you're going to put in them.

- Trash—any item you don't need or want, but whose condition makes it unfit for sale or donation. If something is broken, but could be fixed by someone interested in fixing it, put it in the next container.
- Donate/Sell—items you can't use but someone else can. What to donate and what to sell? Decide that later.
- Store—here's the container for items you can't part with, but don't need frequently or on a regular basis. You're going to regroup the contents of this container later into categories of similar things, so don't worry right now about putting the out-of-season clothes in their own pile.
- Put back—items you need on a regular basis, but which don't seem to have a routine "roost." These are things essential to the room, items you use daily. Make sure you really need them so they don't become clutter in a couple of weeks. Don't plan now where you'll put them. That comes later. Just get them in the box or bin.

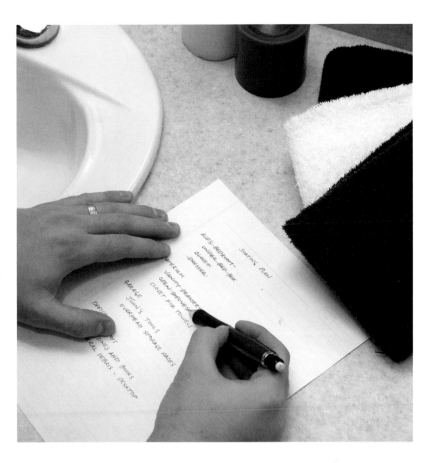

Start sorting

When you get started, make sure you have enough time to get through at least several sections of a room (better yet, an entire room). As you work through each section, be objective about which container is right for each item. Ruthlessness is a good quality in this task. If an item doesn't have a special use, and you haven't seen or touched it in 6 months, it's a good candidate for one of the first three boxes. If you find a decision difficult, you may need a fifth container marked "Uncertain." That's OK—just don't pile these "undecideds" somewhere else in the room. Get them in a container. Taking a break is OK too. But when you return, stick with the section you've been working on. If a container starts to overflow, get another one and label it too.

Ask the right questions

To get items out of the formless mass of clutter and in the right containers, you have to ask the right questions. Tough questions. "Do I really need this?" "Have I used this in the past year?" "Could I get another one, if I needed it?" "Do I have more than one of these?" "Can someone else use it?" Work as hard as you can to make that "toss" pile a big one. Excess goods get in the way of having things that you do use where you can easily see and find them.

The sorting post-op

As soon as you've finished a room, seal up the trash container and move it to the garage or out to the street for collection. The same goes for the sale/donate items.

Find one corner in the garage or basement for all the sale boxes, another corner for the undecided containers, and a third for the boxes marked store. Then repeat this sorting process in the next room, either now or on another day. When the whole house is sorted, look around, sit down, and rest on your laurels for a bit. In a week or so, revisit the undecided boxes and resort them. Resist the temptation to plunge into the designated storage containers. Make plans first about where things should go. For this you need the information on the following pages.

Make it fun

Clutter causes stress, and although uncluttering your space will remove some of the stress in your life, the task itself can be nerve-racking. Set the stage for having fun. Play your favorite music. Work efficiently but not frantically. Invite a friend to help you tackle your closet and offer to reciprocate the next week. A sorting project can make for some great laughs and good talk time. Besides, good friends often know your interests, habits, and stuff better than you do—they can be objective about your mess because they're not attached to it.

 GOOD IDEA

CLEAN OUT DAY
Make uncluttering and organizing a fun family event. Hold a family "clean-out day" a couple of times a year. Once you decide you're going to do this, post it on the calendar right away.

Exit moves: Choose what works for you

Now that you've isolated the items you no longer need, it's time to move them out of your home. The sooner, the better. Any one of several options will help this stuff make its exit. You can sell items individually, you can sell them collectively, or you can donate them.

Call the classifieds

Classified newspaper ads, Internet ads, and Internet auctions are all excellent venues for selling items individually. They are especially useful for antiques and vintage goods. Dealers and collectors will often pay a good price for furnishings, china, silver, and collectibles. Then there's the other stuff that's not antique but still has value. Don't conclude that just because you don't want it, nobody else does either. Remember the adage, "One man's trash is another man's treasure."

Host a yard sale

If the idea of pulling in some extra cash moves you to action, join forces with neighbors or friends, or sell your stuff solo. Set it out on tables, or even on the lawn, tape prices to each item, put up a YARD SALE sign, and watch your goods go. You can advertise in newspapers and shoppers, but the expenses will eat into your profits, so think twice about doing so. If you have lots of stuff, it might be worth it. In any case, post lots of signs around the neighborhood.

Donate and take the deduction

If you don't have the patience for a garage sale—donate your castoffs to a charitable organization and deduct the value on your taxes. Get a copy of the Internal Revenue Service "Determining the Value of Donated Property" (www.irs.gov). Jot down what you're donating, note the values using the IRS publication, and snap a couple of photos of the pile (as backup proof, just to be sure). Call one of the thrift stores in town and arrange a pickup for the goods, get a receipt from the driver, and drop the receipt and photos in your tax file for the year.

"But this might fit some day..."

Lots of us have trouble sorting clothing. The guideline that says "If you haven't worn it for a year, toss!" works for everyday clothing, but it's difficult to heed if you have classic pieces, formalwear, or sets that allow for weight swings. Lessen your closet's load by using it only for garments you'll wear this season. Store the others on a rolling garment rack farther away.

Find out what you really wear this way: Hang all your clothing with the end of the hanger loop facing you. When you've worn an item, replace it on the rod with the loop in the opposite direction. You'll quickly see what items you wear and what hangs waiting. Rather than keep items you hope to return to when you've lost weight, get rid of them now and reward yourself with a new wardrobe for the new you.

Donate and skip the deduction

Don't want to inventory what you're donating, but you want others to have the option to use the goods? Call the thrift store for the pickup and get rid of the stuff—to someone else who can use it.

Pitch it

If the thought of selling your excess stuff, donating it to a thrift store, or giving it away to family and friends is just too much—then give it all the heave-ho and set your boxes and bags out with the trash.

Selling by the neighborhood

A neighborhood garage sale can be a more effective vehicle for selling excess goods than a solo sale. The more stuff, the merrier, as it were. A larger volume of items will tend to draw a larger crowd of buyers. Make your own part of the sale prep easy by designating a shelf in your garage for sale items. Keep sale gear (price stickers and markers) on the shelf. Each time you add an item to the shelf, mark it with your name and a price. Keep a running list so you'll have it after the sale. Come sale time, your items are ready to go!

Preparing for a garage sale

Garage sales can be a barrel of fun—and profitable—but successful sales do not happen by accident. Plans and preparations go a long way to make sure you get a decent return and have fun at the same time.

- Pricing—If you don't know what price to put on an item, start with about one-half to two-thirds of what the item would cost new. If you don't think the item will sell at this price, lower it a little. If you feel you're cheating yourself, raise the price a little. But remember—the main goal of this sale is to get rid of everything. Bring in a friend with garage sale experience to help you decide how much people are willing to pay. Set the price and establish a bottom line. Many people will expect to haggle a little. If you have items you don't think will sell by themselves, throw them in a box and sell the box at one price.

- Marketing—If you have numerous items, it may pay to advertise in the newspaper and shoppers (they're less expensive). This way you might attract that circle of garage salers that every town has—people that might not otherwise be aware of your sale. If your community allows it (and some don't), put up posters large enough to be read from the street. Tack them to telephone poles or to boxes weighted down to keep them from blowing away.

- Organize—In the retail sales business, "Presentation is everything"— and it's no less true for a garage sale. Sweep the floor and cut the grass. Set your sales goods out on tables as attractively as possible. Group like items, such as childrens' things, kitchen utensils, and tools. Isolate special items in a space of their own, so they don't get lost in the crowd of less expensive things. When a sale creates an empty space, move something into that space so it can be better seen. If you're running the sale with other neighbors, make sure you have a list of each neighbor's items. Mark the amount you sold each item for so you can settle up accurately at the end of the day. Make sure each neighbor retrieves unsold items, or have a contingency plan if they don't come for them until later.

- Plan for the future—If you think you'll have another sale in the future, or that they will become a regular feature of your lifestyle, put forth a little extra public relations effort. Serve coffee and donuts. Let the kids have a lemonade stand. Help customers carry their purchases to their cars. People will remember these extra little touches when they see your ad or your sale posters next time.

Storage—It's personal

So now, if you've been following the method described on the previous pages, you're down to one set of boxes—the ones you marked for storage. Before you unpack these boxes, there are tips on the following pages that will make storing this stuff—and solving future storage problems—easier.

What's most important, however, is that you find the solutions that fit your space and your preferences. Storage solutions are often presented as prescriptions—as if one pill cures all storage maladies. Not so. Storage is personal. Find the solutions you're comfortable with. If you don't, you'll be back to the clutter in no time.

First a few principles. Then some practical solutions.

▲ **Different types of storage will often work together in the same space. Kitchens contain good examples of this cooperation, with cabinets and drawers providing closed storage and countertops and open shelves for items you need more often or wish to display.**

The principles of savvy storage

- Keep frequently needed stuff close to where you'll use it—in the room of its primary use—and easy to get to (either in plain sight or on waist-high to eye-level shelves). Store items used less often in another room or in less accessible spots (on top shelves or in the back reaches of the closet). If you have some items—maybe a vacuum cleaner or picnic supplies—that spend more time in a temporary spot than their storage location, that's your hint they need to be closer to where you use them.
- Group like items. Get all the holiday decorations together, all the gift wrap supplies in a box, all sports gear on the same shelves, and all the tools near the work table.
- Label! Slap labels on your bins, baskets, and shelving units; make a habit of referring to that container or location with its name. Telling a family member to look for a new gadget on the shop shelf is much easier than saying it's in "the first cabinet in the garage, third shelf." Assign specific uses for cabinets, closets, and shelves and label those too. Leave the labels up for a few weeks till everyone gets used to the new organization.
- Ditch convention—find sensible locations. If the bathroom closet on the first floor is the make-sense spot for your bucket of tools, so be it.
- Carve out in-transition spots. Assign one surface in your home as a "shipping and receiving" station—a table or shelf on which you can drop off things temporarily when going in and out of the house. Things on that surface will remind you that they belong elsewhere, when you can get to them. Just don't let them linger.
- Create grab 'n' go solutions! For example, store stuff that leaves the house in tote bags in the bags themselves. This eliminates pack-unpack steps for toiletries that always go to the gym, crayons and caps for day-camp, soccer or hockey gear—whatever stuff you can consider regular traveling companions.
- Know what you're willing to walk for. In any given location, there's only so much up-close space. In a kitchen, for example, some people would rather have pots and pans near the sink and don't mind hiking to the garage pantry for foodstuff. Others like the reverse. Respect your preferences, or whatever you've fetched from afar isn't likely to return and will linger on the countertop or table.
- Plan ahead—you'll need storage in the future. Right now not every empty space has to have something in it. Leave some open areas for next year.

Types of storage

You might guess that within the field of storage there are subcategories all their own. Use them in combination with one another to make your storage solutions flexible and effective.

Open storage—Think display when conceiving of open storage. What goes in open storage are things you use and need easy access to, and things you may not use but like looking at. You can create open storage with bookcases, shelves, hall trees, hooks, glass-front cabinets, and any horizontal surface.

Closed storage—This kind of storage keeps things out of sight. It's ideal for things that make a room look cluttered—clothes, kitchen gear, or office supplies. You can further organize the small stuff you keep behind closed

▲ Open storage requires attention to organization to keep its contents from looking jumbled or cluttered.

▲ Remote storage frees up space in the areas you most need it. Keep seasonal items out of the way in the garage, attic, or basement—any location removed from the room in which you'll eventually use the items.

doors with bins, baskets, and dividers. Closets, armoires, cupboards, chests—anything with a door or lid creates closed storage (even skirted tables and boxes under the bed).

Convenient storage—This is storage that's close at hand. It's for the things you need more or less or a regular basis—items you need in the room in which you store them. In a bedroom, closets are examples of convenient storage. In a kitchen, the cupboards or a pot rack are. When space is limited, put the items you use most often in the most convenient spot—the top dresser drawers, for example, not the lower ones.

Remote storage—This is storage that's not in the room in which you use its contents. In fact, remote storage is often the only use for the space it occupies—corners of the garage, attic, or basement. This is where seasonal clothing goes, as well as holiday decorations, baseball gear in the hockey season, and files you need—but not today.

Put your stuff in its place and you'll have more time for doing what you love.

What's your storage style?

Answering the following questions will help you create storage solutions that fit your personal style.

1. Do you need to see your things to remember where they are? _____
2. Would you forget your favorite sweater in a dresser drawer? _____
3. Can you remember what's behind a closed door? _____
4. Does it annoy you to see all your kitchen tools, even if they hang neatly from a wall rack on the backsplash? _____
5. Do your answers to 1 and 3 vary by room? _____

Find your own storage style and work with it, not against it. Doing what's natural to you helps make storage easy. Most people fall into one of the following categories.

See-ers. If you answered yes to questions 1 and 2, you need to see things in order to know where they are. Transparent tubs and wire drawers will help you create order. Naming cupboards and labeling containers will go a long way toward helping you too. Try mounting a row of hooks in any room you find yourself leaving things out (of order). Hanging fabric organizers can also help you create open shelflike spaces in your closet. Most children are visual. You can encourage good organizational skills by labeling shelves and bins and dresser drawers for them.

Knowers. If you answered yes to questions 3 and 4, you likely feel best with belongings tucked away, leaving a few chosen pieces out for viewing. You're able to remember what's in drawers, closets, and opaque tubs. Wire closet drawers might annoy you—so opt for melamine! If open shelving units lined with tubs still strike you as disorderly, replace the shelves with tall cabinets.

Hybrids. An adult storage style generally favors one approach, but can be a hybrid of the two, depending on the room and how much space is devoted to storage. Both types do better with clutter cleared away. And both feel better with like items grouped, corralled, labeled, and stored in named spaces (see "The principles of savvy storage," opposite).

Making storage

Imagine this for a bit: Empty your home of all your belongings, then gut the house of all its closets, cabinetry, and furnishings, leaving only the walls, floors, and ceilings. Bring the belongings back in and you'd be hard-pressed to store them—no boxes, bins, baskets or tubs allowed—in any organized fashion. You'd have to make the storage you need. Here are the most common implements that make storage.

■ Hooks create order, open up floor space, and make use of vertical surfaces (or the undersides of shelving) so things aren't in the way. Hooks solve an enormous number of storage puzzles. Visual types love hooks for creating order within view. The pegboard is a hook-lovers' dream—put one here today, there tomorrow. It can extend the usefulness of the hook to include shelves, bins, or jars. Frame it, paint it, do an entire wall in pegboard. New pegboard systems resemble paneling—a perfect feature for a family or living room.

▲ The shelf also opens up floor space, but for items hooks won't hold. Shallow shelves can be especially useful for small items—the key is to hang shelves just a little deeper than what's on them. Too deep and they quickly morph into caves.

While you're looking up for shelf space, aim high. Shelves hung 12 to 18 inches below the ceiling or above windows make good display space for collectibles, family photos, and anything you like to look at but don't need routine access to. See pages 156–157 to learn how to install various kinds of wall shelving.

▲ Cubbies, nooks, and crannies open up floor space and open up wall space too. They make the perfect solution in bathrooms for convenient storage of items that get daily use but that you need "out of the way." Don't overlook their potential for creating dramatic display space in living room and family room walls. You can easily open up a nook or cranny in an existing wall and finish it to provide display shelving.

▶ The pullout is a shelf on wheels. Thanks to pullouts, goods you'd have to root around for in the depths of a space roll right into view. A drawer is a pullout and so is a tub on a shelf. Cabinetmakers and storage manufacturers have embraced pullout power to yield pullout cupboards, pantry sections, and even carts that roll out from understair space to make it useful.

▲ Rings and rods are essentially a variation of the hook. They get things off the floor and make storage stylish and easy accessible. Closet rods go hand in hand with a moveable form of the hook—the hanger—providing organization, convenience, and portability.

Tool time

You can install 95 percent of all storage implements using just a few basic tools, and you don't need super skills to use them. Chances are you already have many of them in drawers or in the garage—drill and bits, level, hammer, punch, screwdrivers, tape measure, and stud finder. Gather them into a bucket and start solving your storage issues.

■ Containers—tubs, baskets, hassocks, boxes, and bins—keep things corralled in one place. They work to contain items in out-of-the-way spots and to keep items for daily use readily at hand. Hide them from view or use them to embellish the design scheme of a room. Sturdy lids allow stacking. Label them and locating things becomes a cinch. Opaque or transparent, tubs are easy to wipe clean.

Retrofit or renovate?

There's almost always a way to squeeze more storage space into any room. It's all a matter of putting wasted space to work and then breaking the space and the goods into manageable pieces. A few extra shelves, some racks, baskets, and hooks, and you're on your way. Many commercial storage implements are available for a quick retrofit that will add to your storage capacity. More extensive changes call for renovation.

▲ Drawer dividers can be purchased and cut or arranged to suit your stash of flatware, tools, or small ingredients. Two levels help take advantage of deeper drawers.

▲ **Build in your backsplash.** Call on your favorite handyperson to build towel holders and ledges for spices, tea and coffee makings, even mugs along your backsplash wall. As a less expensive alternative, hang backsplash baskets. Mount racks for frequently used tools such as utensils. Some racks have small baskets for smaller seasonings or gear. Buy or build a 3- or 4-inch shallow ledge for the back of your counter—use it for frequently used oils, seasonings, mugs. Go narrower for spice containers.

▶ To tuck things under cabinets—paper towel holders, coffeemakers, and undercabinet radio fittings, all you need is a drill and a screwdriver. Some baskets, such as knife and spice racks, are even hinged. Pull them down for use, push them back up and they're out of sight. If wire baskets clash with your kitchen style, hide them. Tambou-doors make great coverups for everyday small appliances. Make the space work even harder by screwing in a 3- to 4-inch shelf, or two, overhead for condiments, creamers, and cups. Then slip on a couple of baskets to store filters and lids and a wire shelf for lower-profile appliances.

 Add a shelf. Transform a vacant door surface into storage space by adding a hanging shelf. The back of a base cabinet door is the perfect place to keep cleaning supplies and other items from cluttering up your kitchen or vanity countertop. Commercial units come complete with brackets and hardware and are made for virtually every door style and dimension. Basic tools do the job.

▲ Pullouts bring contents into the light with ready-to-install pullout baskets, available in one-, two-, and three-tier models, some with half shelves to fit around plumbing.

Use inexpensive solutions for the short term or as a way to test a storage method that you'll upgrade later.

GOOD IDEA

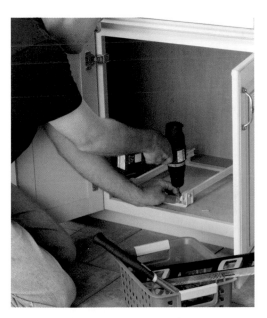

SHELF SMARTS

Most upper cabinets arrive with just two shelves. Add one or two and you'll avoid stacking dishes too high. Purchase the shelves from a cabinet supplier or have a home center cut melamine or wood to fit.

■ Use your tool kit to upgrade your cabinetry in minutes. Installing a roll-out feature, such as this trash container, requires only basic tools and basic skills.

▲ Conscript the back of a closet in one room for open storage in an adjacent room. This combination of open and closed storage units occupies space in what was formerly an oversize bedroom closet. While you're at it, run the wall cabinets to the ceiling—a much better and more attractive use of space than a soffit.

▲ Use renovation as an opportunity to create space with a style all its own. Here, this minimalist vanity with a hint of Asian style establishes a mood that's quietly functional. The hanging cabinet seems suspended on the wall, adding to the light, airy feeling in this modern bathroom.

▶ Bathrooms, especially those in older homes, are notoriously small and often do not lend themselves to effective expansion. Incorporating built-in dividers in cabinet drawers will keep small items orderly while taking advantage of all of the available space.

▶ Open shelves benefit from pullouts too. Line shelving with baskets, and you've essentially put together a pullout system, minus the gliding hardware. Many homeowners choose this option simply for the visual interest and texture that baskets add to a room.

GOOD IDEA

Get vertical. Screw vertical wire dividers between base-cabinet shelves to store baking sheets, muffin tins, trays, and platters.

Pullouts. Baskets and lightly loaded jelly roll pans can serve as pullouts, even sturdy grocery boxes cut to a few inches of their base make effective pullouts!

Overhead space. Run a display ledge over the top of your doors, windows, and cabinets—or just use your cabinet tops—to display personal collections or bulky cooking gear (if you don't mind stretching from a stool to retrieve things).

Shelf-bottom hangers. You'll gain shelf space, upside-down style, when you screw goblet racks or cup hooks into a shelf bottom.

Skirt the issue. The space under a table harbors great storage opportunities, and you can hide the stuff you put under it with a skirt you make from fabric that fits the decor of the room. If you don't have a table in mind for this option, buy an unfinished round or rectangular table at your home center. Decorate the top with a homemade mosaic and fasten the skirting to the edge with hook-and-loop fasteners.

Under the bed. Measure the space from the bottom of the bed frame to the floor and between the legs. Get clear plastic containers that will slide in and out easily.

At your feet. Put the toe-kicks under kitchen base cabinets to work by adding pullout drawers. Install touch-release latches so you can open them with a tap of your toe.

Grab garage space. Even in small garages, there's usually enough room to hang a wall cabinet in front of the car.

◀ **Bare wall space is a clue there's a storage opportunity just waiting to happen.** This pantry was created from part of the closet space in an adjoining room with the help of some moderate renovation and wire shelving. Similar narrow storage space with wood shelves can be built into existing walls between the studs.

▶ **Islands are excellent for making sure you get the most out of your kitchen space,** putting to good use that often empty central floor area. Make your island more useful by adding open storage to one side as shown here. If your budget won't permit a full-scale renovation with matching island, or if the kitchen doesn't provide enough room, get a rolling island or butcher block on wheels so you can move it to a side wall when it's not needed.

Secure storage

Valuables and dangerous goods—jewelry, firearms, toxic materials, and tools—need to be stored away from prying eyes and those who'd misuse (or misappropriate) them.

Jewelry and small valuables. Home centers and locksmiths carry fireproof safes with key or combination locks in portable and wall-mounted styles. A portable safe is fine for protecting your goods from fire and water damage, but doesn't protect them from burglary. Wall-mounted safes are available, and although heavier models require structural supports, they offer more deterrence to the more diligent thieves, who can cut a light safe from the wall as easily as you can install one.

Firearms. Store firearms in locked units manufactured specifically for this purpose, with ammunition stored and locked separately. Common sense prevails here—the location of the units and the keys are best not discussed widely, and keys should be kept out of sight.

Toxic materials. Cleaning solvents, garden chemicals, paint supplies, and gas and oil for yard tools should be stored on shelves out of reach, behind locked doors. Store flammable goods away from high heat.

Tools. Be mindful of children who might wander into your shop. An unwitting tug on the cord of a drill resting on the table can mean a heavy blow to the curious child below. Put tools away to prevent accidents. Fit your shop with a locked door.

Systematize your spaces

ustom-built, made-to-fit solutions—today, custom solutions are within everyone's reach. Lumber and hardware are now joined by a growing array of easy-to-install, multifunctional storage systems (some handily cut to size) that you can mix, match, or modify to meet your specific needs. Plan and install the solutions yourself, or take advantage of home center services that will design and/or install them for you.

These storage systems are available in a range of prices, designs, finishes, and quality levels. Here are the major system types that you'll find in home centers.

Melamine

This material is the next toughest thing to solid, finished wood (such high quality wood can be too costly for storage uses). Shelf, drawer, and cupboard surfaces in melamine systems feature a layer of resin thermally fused to particleboard. The result is a hard, damage-resistant surface that cleans easily. Higher end melamine systems use ¾-inch board, less costly systems use ⅝-inch board. Melamine is sold in whites, and sometimes in black and wood-grain patterns.

Wire

Affordable, lightweight, easy to haul and install, and warp-resistant—these qualities have made vinyl- and epoxy-coated steel closet systems wildly popular. Slotted and mesh designs allow air to circulate—that's good—and small items to drop through—that can be a problem. Solving drop-through is easy, however—just purchase clear shelf and drawer liners. Fans of vinyl say it's more resistant to rust. Fans of epoxy report that it doesn't get sticky in humid settings. You'll find wire-based systems sold with white finishes, increasingly in silver-tone nickel finishes, and in an industrial looking gray.

Wood

If you love the look of wood, look for it in high-end closet systems, expandable pantry shelving units, and wine racks. Most units come with their side panels predrilled so you can put the shelves where you want them. If you're handy and possess woodworking skills, you can, of course make your own. But expect to pay a premium for hardwood materials, and if you have immediate storage needs, this may not be the best option. If your budget has enough room for wood in the first place, it's quicker and easier to use a custom prefabricated system.

BUYER'S GUIDE

CHOOSING A STORAGE SYSTEM

When choosing a storage system, check out these aspects before you buy.

Fixed or adjustable? To what extent can you reposition shelves or rods? Exchange drawer sizes? Does a fixed setup work for you, or will you want the flexibility to rearrange it to meet future needs?

Wall-mounted or floor-based? Storage systems can be secured in many ways. Wall-mounted systems keep floors free for vacuuming. Floor-based options look more like furniture, which some buyers prefer.

Load capacity. Check the load-bearing capacity of a shelving unit. It's generally noted on the package. When in doubt, buy more capacity than you think you'll need. Buy too little and the shelves will eventually sag.

▲ No two closets are the same, and almost all closet systems can be tailored to spaces of any size and shape. Starter sets are designed to meet basic needs and be ready for expansion when you are. Some come precut to your specs, others you'll have to cut yourself. Most brands feature specialty add-ons for ties, belts, shoes, and other accessories.

◄ Opportunities abound for systematizing storage in your kitchen pantry. Wire racks, shelves, baskets, and pullouts for recycling, food storage, and kitchen supplies are available to suit your needs.

🚫 **SAFETY ALERT**

Shim freestanding storage units so they stand level and fasten their tops to the wall with L-brackets to prevent toppling.

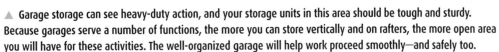

▲ Garage storage can see heavy-duty action, and your storage units in this area should be tough and sturdy. Because garages serve a number of functions, the more you can store vertically and on rafters, the more open area you will have for these activities. The well-organized garage will help work proceed smoothly—and safely too.

The attractive factor

Tood looks are inspiring. A good-looking storage solution inspires its own upkeep. That means when you like the looks of your storage solutions, you'll maintain them. A pretty painted closet with strong, sturdy, and attractive hangers won't be ignored or trashed. The same goes for a tidy garage or utility room with stacks of plastic tubs in a couple of energizing colors, or a kitchen fitted with organizers in red, white, and chrome. Keep that in mind and think twice before you bring home another buff, drab, or dull storage piece. Plan your storage with an eye to what you like to see. Even if you don't go for careful coordination, choose storage gear in fresh white (it looks crisp, washes well), basic black (doesn't show scuff marks, looks classic), or colors that please you.

Don't underestimate the power of good looks—or a great color—to inspire order. When you like the way your storage looks, you're more likely to keep it up.

▲ In this kitchen renovation, the entire arts and crafts theme (with a nod to contemporary colors) is carried out in great detail to match the architecture of the original built-in divider on the right. When your kitchen cabinets—or storage in any other room for that matter—looks this attractive, you'll want to make sure there's no surrounding clutter to detract from its appearance.

Don't hunt—make labels work

It's a fact—slap a label on your boxes, bins, and tubs and name your drawers, closets, shelves, and stash spots, and storage gets easier. Use labels and names and you will be:

■ More likely to remember where things are located
■ More likely to return things to their proper place
■ Less likely to stash stuff somewhere "just because"

Have fun! Naming your stash spots and labeling locations gives you a chance to create your own family lingo. Put your artistic (and perhaps messy) child in charge of designing or lettering your labels. Get the kids involved and you'll encourage some good organizational habits too. Do allow a tub and shelf here and there to be labeled "Miscellaneous."

Getting the job done

Solving storage problems in some cases is as simple as putting up a few wire shelves. In most cases, however, creating good storage solutions is a multistep process (and this comes after you've sorted your stuff and gotten rid of things you don't need). Here are the steps involved:

- Evaluate potential storage options (including retrofitting or renovating rooms).
- Assign specific uses to existing storage space—cabinets, closets, and shelves. (Stick with these assignments. Don't let socks creep into the drawer for sheets and linens.)
- Prioritze the location of storage according to frequency of use.
- Categorize everything.
- Plan for future storage needs. If any of your storage needs—present or future—calls for installation or construction, you have several options.

Almost all discussions about storage assume that storage units will be permanent. Sometimes, however, you need temporary storage to get you by. Metal or plastic garment racks on casters roll where they're needed to provide hanging space in a guest room, for a party, for out-of-season clothes, or for a garage sale. Unfinished wooden shelving swallows masses of out-of-season clothing or pantry goods. Slip a loosely fitted muslin cover over temporary racks or shelves—make your own covers or buy them—and you might find their bare-bones look appealing enough to make them permanent.

Do all of it yourself

Arm yourself with just eight basic tools, as described on page 15, and you will be able to install 95 percent of all storage solutions.

Do part of it yourself

Divide the work into two categories—tasks you can accomplish yourself and tasks you need help with. Hire a handyperson to do what you're not inclined to. For example, hire someone to retrofit shelving in your vintage armoire, then do the finish work—paint or stain—yourself.

Hire a handyperson to do all of it

Even if you can hang your own shelves and closet systems, sometimes the job gets done more quickly if someone else does it. In two or three hours, a handyperson can have several storage solutions up and running. Handyfolks are capable of constructing a broad range of made-to-fit storage solutions, from standing shelf units to rollout features for kitchen cabinets.

Go to the experts

Your closet's a mess? You don't know how to begin making sense of your garage? Go to a pro. Professional closet and organizing experts are joining kitchen and bath designers to bring insight and solutions to home storage puzzles. You can hire an architect or independent designer and pay a large fee, but there's plenty of good help available either free or for a small design fee. Retailers who sell storage products and systems, and kitchen and bath products, increasingly employ designers to serve their customers—often with no obligation to buy. Of course they solve your problems with products their employers sell. If you go this route, ask the designer for references and photos. These can give you a sense of how they work and how well they tailor solutions to individual needs.

Entries and mudrooms

Entries and mudrooms are the first places family or visitors see when they enter the house, but they're often the last spaces to gain attention when it comes to organizing their contents. These rooms are probably used more frequently than others in the house, but because you only use them as passageways, you don't often take the time to get them in "storage shape." They quickly become a tangle of possessions. The problem can compound itself in winter climates, adding jackets, scarves, boots, and heavy clothes to the array of stuff an entry must contain.

A well-organized entry gets your day off to a good start. It may seem inconsequential if you have to spend a few extra moments fishing for the car keys, but those moments start your day with stress. If you can rid your morning schedule of such frantic searches, you can head off in a more productive direction right from the start.

Entry spaces act as transition areas for the family and are also one of the more public spaces of your home. A junked-up front entry can create a disorderly impression in the minds of guests, a messy environment that might have become so habitual you don't even notice it. It's like an inadvertent sign that says "hazardous conditions ahead." You might think, "Well, that mess . . . that's not really me." Fact is, however, it is you—but you can change it.

Entries are small, and the task of turning them into well-oiled departure spots and landing pads is best accomplished by removing everything from the area and sizing things up. You may be amazed at how big a pile this makes, but with everything out of the way you can assess your storage needs and begin to plan new solutions.

Chapter 2 highlights

ENTRY STRATEGIES
It's not about getting in and out, it's about not leaving a trail in the process.

26

FRONT ENTRIES AND FOYERS
Front entries are for the family and the public. They let you in and out of the house, but they are also the first place a visitor sees when entering your home.

28

BACK DOORS AND MUDROOMS
You can breathe a little easier in the design of your back door mudroom, without letting it become, well, a mudroom.

30

STASHES FOR SMALL STUFF
Stashes for the small things you need when you leave the house each day are perhaps the most important storage places of all.

32

Entry strategies

Even though entries are almost always smaller than other rooms in the house, their very size seems to limit storage opportunities. That makes them difficult to tackle. But straightening out an entry becomes easier with a little strategy. Here's how:

Categorize. First get everything out of the room and sort it into categories—one pile for what you absolutely must have in the room, another for things you need for convenience, and a third for seasonal stuff. Move the seasonal stuff to the back closet or other remote storage location, and move on to the next step.

Assess and measure. Look at the empty space and inventory potential storage locations. There's the closet, of course, but how about the wall? Can you hang hooks on it or move in a hall chest (it not only has drawers for storage, its top might be perfect for keys, mail, and cell phones). What about stylish narrow cupboards? Or shelves? Or a vertical cabinet with doors? Measure the space to make sure your solutions will fit and draw a plan of any renovations you decide to install.

Shop around for the new items you need—you want your storage to be stylish. Then install the storage solutions yourself or hire the work out to a pro.

■ Closed storage (above) is essential in an entryway. It will keep this small space from cluttering with things that need to be there, but don't need to be readily available. Hooks (even in the closet recesses) need to be there too. This unit combines these solutions into one installation. A message center (left) isn't a storage structure as such, but it helps tie on-the-go families together and keeps their activities organized.

The systematic entryway

Think of the entries to your home as a balanced combination of space and system. Too much of one or the other and the room becomes dysfunctional. Here's the minimum collection of storage implements you need to get in and out of the house smoothly.

Hanging space. That's hooks or hangers for jackets, coats, hats, and umbrellas.

Loading docks, large and small. You, your family, and visitors need a surface on which to set purses, packs, gym bags, and laptops plus any other items that are on their way in or out. Your "docks" can be open to view, partially concealed in baskets, bins, and tubs, or behind a door.

Drawers, "minidressers," baskets. Place them or other small containers on a shelf, table, hall stand, or chest for wallets, keys, and combs. You don't have to stop and open a drawer to get at their contents—just grab 'n' go.

Electric outlets. For cell phones that need recharging.

Mailbox. Trays, baskets, boxes, anything big enough to handle the mail (no lids please). You'll need one for incoming and outgoing mail.

Mirror. For those last-minute grooming checks.

Memo board. This can be a dry-erase board, corkboard, chalkboard, or just a clothespin squeezing paper notes on the edge of a basket.

▶ Closet organizing systems are made for more than bedroom use. They can quickly turn a crowded front closet into a smoothly working space that makes exit and entry convenient. If your front closet has the space, make it a his-and-hers location that keeps each person's clothes in its own place.

▲ Cubbies can provide a stylish solution that corrals items—mail, newspapers, and magazines—on a horizontal surface and still provides easy access to them.

💡 GOOD IDEA

THE VINTAGE CLOSET
Turn a vintage or new armoire into a coat closet for your front entry. Deck it out with ventilated wire shelving for school-age children. A closet rod provides a spot for hanging coats, but hooks would serve as well. Laundry baskets beneath the bottom shelf will swallow packs and sporting equipment; fit each door with mirror, memo board, and a little tray or holder for supplies. Give each child a place for small essentials by placing a plastic tool box, see-through box, plastic stacking shelves, or minidresser on the lower shelf. If the kids are carrying cell phones, slip the charger cords through a cutout in the back of the armoire.

Front entries and foyers

2

PREPARING FOR INSTALLATION

I s it easy for you to collect all your things and get out the door in the morning? Do you or family members run back inside to fetch forgotten items? Does returning home create a mess that you have to clean up? Fine-tune your front entry with solutions that work for your family.

Every sound storage solution simplifies your life, but the ability of your front foyer, back door mudroom, or garage door off the kitchen to make departures and arrivals hassle-free is something you'll appreciate several times each day.

Entries that work well offer a visual "welcome home" while putting coats and gloves, purses and packs, briefcases, laptops, and gym bags—not to mention wallets, keys, loose change, pagers, and cell phones—in order.

The solutions on these pages include but aren't limited to entry locations. The art of creating orderly exits and entries can extend to other rooms as well.

 GOOD IDEA

TREE OR TANGLE?
To keep the hall tree from becoming a stalactite formation of clothing, reserve its use just for guests.

▲ It doesn't have to be fancy, but a hall chest can hold a lot of stuff you need in the entry that you don't need routine access to. Drawers, however, are a great way to create an internal mess. Rooting around in their contents for something you need can be frustrating, especially when the school bus is waiting on the street. Keep the drawers organized with smaller containers, such as baskets or bins. Even shoe boxes will do for temporary subdividers.

◄ Whether in a front entry or a mudroom, wherever boots are going on and coming off some kind of seat makes this chore a whole lot easier. The seat can provide hooked storage above with lidded closed storage or divided open storage below.

COPING WITH THE CRAMPED COAT CLOSET

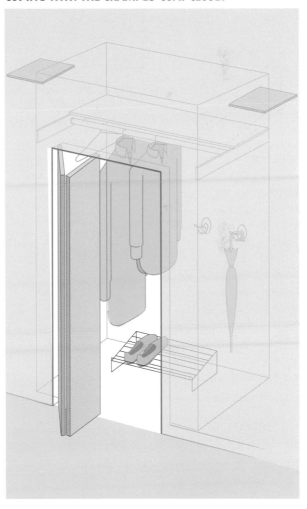

▲ Here's a foyer table that demonstrates how thinking outside the box can create storage solutions that are both fun and functional. This commercial baker's rack turned into a foyer table uses acrylic plastic sheets to keep small items from falling through. Always let the style of your house, especially the adjoining rooms, guide your decisions about the style of a storage unit.

▲ Coat closets in older homes can be frustratingly small, but you can improve their efficiency with a few small changes. Set a closet system wire rack on the floor to raise boots and shoes and make them easier to retrieve. Replace the heavy hinged door with bifold or pocket doors. You might gain a few inches of space, but even if you don't, your new doors will provide easier access. Extend the top shelf around the sides, but make them narrower or they will interfere with access to hanging clothes. Add hooks in the back or sides for thin items like umbrellas.

Back doors and mudrooms

GOOD IDEA

BUY OR MAKE?
You can buy commercially produced bins, baskets, tubs, and trays, but you can employ homemade substitutes just as well. Especially in mudrooms primarily designed for kids, use shoe boxes, decorated cans, or plastic food storage units.

Despite their humble name, and back door location, mudrooms can be quite elaborate—closet rooms with fixed shelves and dividers for all the gear we come and go with, all dressed up with arches and trim. On the other hand, mudrooms can be quite plain: A shelf, a rod, or series of hooks, a knee-level shelf for packs and packages, a low bench, and a handful of baskets at several levels will keep everything neat and accessible.

Elaborate or simple, costly or cheap, mudrooms that serve best over the years are flexible. Rod, hook, and shelf heights can be adjusted according to the user's height, the types of gear they handle, and the number of people in the household.

▲ Benches and mudrooms go hand in hand. If boots and shoes have to go on and off in the mudroom, you'll certainly want a bench to make this easier. But there's more storage in this bench than meets the eye. Hinge the top and you can hide all sorts of mudroom stuff. Benches are one of the best ways to keep sports gear out sight but accessible. Vertical cabinets also work, of course, but you can't use them to put your boots on. (See pages 176–181 for how to build a bench like this.)

 GOOD IDEA

GREAT MUDROOM MOVES

Some mudroom setups look great at first glance, but are difficult to use. Give some thought to the following factors when you plan yours.

Adjustability. This already mentioned quality—by way of adjustable shelf locations or movable organizers—will make your mudroom flex with your household's needs.

Elbow room. Dividers are not a boon if they cramp your coats or make room for only one and a half pairs of shoes. Consider individually divided spaces for items such as purses and packs, and undivided spaces for other goods (such as those coats).

Accessibility. Prime locations for shelves or bins are at eye, knee, or foot level. If your plans call for overhead storage, save that space for occasionally used items—or someone who can reach it.

Room for pets and pals. If you have a pet, a nanny, or frequent houseguests, plan space and install implements that will handle their things too.

Pullout lower storage, with a lip. Go fancy with a drawer shelf on heavy-duty glides, or plain with a big plastic or wicker laundry basket. The goal is visible, easy-access, contained storage that keeps things in place.

 SAFETY ALERT

DON'T HIT A SNAG
When installing hooks, always plan their location so they won't grab clothes, snag packages, or poke people in the passageway.

Stashes for small stuff

Imagine a smooth, orderly departure from home each morning. No more wasted time running back into the house to retrieve misplaced essentials. The secret is habit—and a dedicated stash spot that's near your most frequently used exit/entry door. Want to step your efficiency up a notch further? Make sure each member of the family has a personal spot.

Your stash spot: public or private?

Before you screw that key rack by the back door, make sure you're comfortable with its visibility. Small children are intrigued by keys and all manner of small things. If your home is a bustling social center, it's quite common for small things to be bumped out of place. Your stash spot might be better located inside a drawer or cupboard a little off the beaten path.

▲ If you carry cell phones or mobile devices, boost the function of your stash spot by planning outlet access. Whatever you use for a cell phone stash, drill a hole in the back for access to outlets for the charger. Drill drawer backs for access in cabinets or the back of the cabinet itself. Add electrical outlets to your closet plans.

Tap tool chests for grab 'n' go stash spots.

 GOOD IDEA

A SMALL-STUFF GARAGE
Include an appliance garage in your entry plans and you can leave it open or shut as you desire.

Small essentials

Here's a representative list of things you'll need to "park" on your way in and out of the house.

- Keys
- Wallet
- Cash
- Cell phone, pager
- PDAs and other mobile devices
- Sunglasses
- Lip balm
- Combs
- Credit cards and more . . .

BEFORE

AFTER

▲ The download drawer is a common feature in most homes. Everyone's got a junk drawer full of odds and ends. Dump the tangled mess and claim the drawer as your stash spot. Line the drawer with kitchen drawer dividers to keep your things visible and tangle-free.

▲ Mudrooms don't have to be large and complicated. A few hours in your workshop with simple tools can produce all the storage you need.

▼ If shelving is your stash surface of choice, add bins, baskets, or other low containers to keep their contents categorized. Otherwise you may end up with a heap of items that are easy to get to but time consuming to unravel, and not very pretty to look at.

◀ If you like the bold clean lines of a utilitarian style, try a classic tool chest for mudroom and entry storage. Use small containers for keys and the things you have to grab by the handful, baskets or trays for the mail and other things you need reminding of. The deep drawers of the tool chest are not only for tools, they're perfect for wrapping paper, mailing supplies, and other things that always end up in some remote location just when you need them.

Bedrooms

Bedrooms are like kitchens. Really—that's not a forced analogy. Bedrooms are like kitchens because they have a large number of jobs to do, all at the same time. They're not only places for sleeping and a haven or getaway, they're also reading rooms, TV and music rooms, dressing rooms, and in some families, a kind of subcenter for family gatherings and summits. Even if they were used only for sleeping and dressing, the amount of bedroom stuff that needs storage is enormous. Because of that, bedrooms are prime

candidates for clutter. After all, what's more convenient than dropping a pile of clothes on the already unmade bed? It looks right at home there.

The problem is, nothing interferes more with the serenity of a bedroom (which is, after all, the one room ordained mostly to this peaceful state) than clutter. So how do you fix this space?

When you think of bedroom storage, your first visualization is probably the closet. That's OK, but if you restrict your options to the closet, you may find it overflowing. Dressers, of course, are

Chapter 3 highlights

COPING WITH CLOSETS
Closets are put there to provide storage solutions, yet they most often become storage problems. What to do about them?

36

CLOSET SYSTEMS
Systematizing a closet space is one solution, and a prevalent one at that. Many products are available to give you a hand.

38

FURNITURE
Furniture is just as viable a storage vehicle as any other you might think of. Don't forget it in the bedroom.

44

CHILDREN'S ROOMS
Kid's rooms have so many jobs to do and so many things in them. A shovel and rake are not the only solutions.

46

the next option and their drawers help free up closet space. There are more. Nightstands, cedar or other kinds of covered chests, open shelving, armoires, and even headboards can help you solve storage problems (and alter the style of your room at the same time). We haven't even gotten to the requirements for your entertainment center and sound system, but if those are additions you plan for your bedroom, you'll need places to park them too.

You can tackle a bedroom storage problem in much the same way as other cluttered rooms—first pull everything out of the closet and dressers and get it in one place. Sort it into piles according to whether its presence is essential, handy, or seasonal. Remove the seasonal goods to a remote storage location, and then assess what you've got left and where you can put it—comfortably. This process is likely to uncover stuff with nowhere to go. You can find solutions to this dilemma on the following pages.

Coping with closets

Closets are the primary storage venue for almost all bedrooms. But just because they're everywhere doesn't mean they all have to look the same. Your goal in gaining control of your closet is to personalize it so it meets your needs. There are so many closet solutions available these days, there isn't any part of this puzzle you can't solve. Even if you may not think so right now, you can get all the parts of your wardrobe to fit comfortably in your closet, from shoes on up.

Designing your closet

To start with, pull out the closet rod—it may get in the way when you are considering a single- or double-rod solution. Make a list of your entire wardrobe, pants, shirts, jackets, blouses, belts, ties, and shoes. Then think rods, hooks, drawers, and shelves, and designate the kinds of structure that best stores each item on your list. Jackets, shirts, pants, and blouses go on rods, but they need only half the vertical space that dresses, robes, and coats do. Consider a double-rod solution—it can open up oodles of unused area—but you'll also need a single rod for the long things. Sweaters, folded jeans, scarves, hats, and caps can go on shelves. So can shoes and other footwear. Ties and belts store well on hooks, along with purses (which are also a candidate for shelving, especially purses without straps). When you've finished assigning a home for everything, you have the beginnings of a plan.

Now inventory your room for available storage space. Sketch out the room and post the measurements of the closet on the sketch. Include measurements of open wall spaces, too, and visualize chests, dressers, and other potential storage solutions in these spaces. Then sketch in the various elements and decide what you can make yourself and what you should purchase.

▲ When you run into a solution that leaves open space where clutter can accumulate, subdivide it with tubs or baskets. Tubs work well for things you don't use often. Baskets you can grab. Remember to keep the least used items toward the rear of the space, the most frequently used toward the front.

◄ This closet storage solution demonstrates how shelves, rods, cubbies, drawers, and hooks all work together to maximize storage and accessibility. First, the two-rod section makes good use of the vertical space needed for shorter clothing items, while the single rod leaves plenty of room for longer dresses and coats. If you have enough closet space, divide it into his and hers sections. Items that see frequent use go in eye-level cubbies and below. Things used occasionally go above.

The well-oiled closet

For a closet to function efficiently, all its parts have to work together. This means allowing enough room for them to do their job.

■ Clothes on hangers need a rod about 12 inches from the wall. For a double-rod system, put the lower rod 42 inches from the floor, the upper rod at 78 to 84 inches, depending on your height.

■ If there's a shelf above, it should clear the rod by 6 inches.

■ Kid's closets work well with the same specs, but plan for a shelf 29 inches from the floor.

Closet systems

1 f you think a closet system (see page 20) is the way to go, first decide whether you want ventilated shelving or wood. Although your choice is largely a matter of personal preference, ventilated shelving allows clothes to breathe, but wood shelving is better for storing small and oddly shaped items (they won't fall through). Wood is also more expensive, so your budget may make the decision for you.

Select the base piece of the system first—the position and installation of most of the remaining pieces will be relative to the base. Even if you're a design whiz, it will pay you (most are free) to use the home center design services specific to your system. You'll get many ideas about how you can make your space efficient—a few you might not have thought of.

Whether you use these services or not, you'll need to know how many hanging items you have or how long a rod space they occupy, as well as the number of pairs of shoes, boxes, and containers, and a rough idea of how much you want to spend.

■ Wire systems range in size and complexity from the basic designs for small reach-in closets to those that will fit large walk-in closets. Some basic systems are truly a closet in a box. Manufacturers use a variety of methods for hanging the shelves. Some rely on brackets that slip into slotted vertical tracks (above). Others use a system of hooks and clips to affix the shelves to the wall (left).

BEDROOMS

■ Like their wire counterparts, wood closet organizing systems can be designed to custom-fit closets of any size and configuration. Each manufacturer makes units that when combined with each other will produce a storage solution tailored to your needs. Melamine is the material of choice for most of these systems, but you can build your closet with a personal arrangement of drawers, open shelves, rods, and cubbies. Planning is the key to designing your system. Pick your starter package first, deciding whether you want a closed or open structure or one that combines the virtues of both.

◄ Even with the most well-designed closet system, you always have items, especially small things, that just don't seem to fit any category. For these you need baskets, bins, or other forms of containment. Choose your containers to match the overall style of your storage system. They provide an excellent way to add dashes of color to your closet, making it more attractive. Containers also keep small things from falling through the spaces in a wire system.

► Don't forget to look up when you're planning your closet system. That empty space above the top shelf may be too high for you to retrieve items for daily use, but it offers an excellent space for storing—and displaying—the more unusual items in your closet, things you like looking at.

 GOOD IDEA

TIPS FOR STORING CLOTHES

■ Silks, laces, and linens belong on padded hangers. Those with a wood frame under the padding will keep the shape of the item better than a wire-core hanger.

■ While you're at it, gather up all the wire hangers from the cleaners and trash or recycle them. They're too thin and weak to be of any use in supporting clothes and you've probably got a handful of them that are just taking up rod space.

■ Wool and knitted items will stretch and become misshapen on hangers. These are things for shelves or drawers. Fold them before you put them up so they'll keep their shape.

■ Remove the plastic bags from clothes just home from the cleaners. The bags trap moisture and the plastic can react

with fumes from the cleaning agent. Let newly cleaned clothes breath a little, then store them in zippered bags. The best bags for this purpose will have vents in the corners to allow air circulation. In a pinch, wrap the clothes in an old bedsheet for temporary storage.

■ If you have things destined for long-term storage, get them dry-cleaned first. This will prevent any stains from setting in the material during storage.

■ Seeking remote storage locations? Avoid a damp basement or unfinished attic. Damp basements can rot or mildew your clothes, and the heat in an unfinished attic can rapidly deteriorate most fabrics.

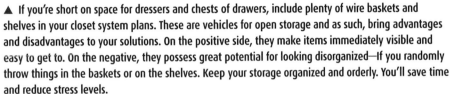

▲ If you're short on space for dressers and chests of drawers, include plenty of wire baskets and shelves in your closet system plans. These are vehicles for open storage and as such, bring advantages and disadvantages to your solutions. On the positive side, they make items immediately visible and easy to get to. On the negative, they possess great potential for looking disorganized—If you randomly throw things in the baskets or on the shelves. Keep your storage organized and orderly. You'll save time and reduce stress levels.

Keeping the moths out

Moth damage is commonly associated with the storage of seasonal (usually woolen) items. But their appetite is not limited to wool in summer. Moths don't know what season it is, and both their larval and adult stages can feast on clothes you use even on a frequent basis. Since they are attracted to grease, food stains, perspiration, and starch, start your mothproofing by brushing woolens after you use them and asking your cleaners to use a cleaning solution that includes a mothproofing agent. You can reduce larval damage by storing your items in a cedar-lined chest or by dropping cedar slats or balls into drawers. Sand the cedar once a year to release fresh oil, or wipe it with bottled cedar oil. Cedar oil won't kill adult moths, however. Only the chemicals in mothballs will—and these are toxic to humans also. When using mothballs, store the items away from areas of daily use and give them a chance to air out before you put them in the closet.

A touch of convenience

3

BEDROOMS

■ Regardless of what kind of commercial closet system you employ, you'll find accessories to store shoes, ties, belts, and hats—all the things that can take over a closet if they don't have a home of their own. Even if you have to forego an accessory specific to the system because it won't fit, you can make do with its "regular" counterpart. For example, all kinds of racks and carriers are made for shoe storage (above left), but regular low shelves will work just fine (left). If you don't have room inside the closet, racks and pocket hangers mounted on the back of a door will do nicely (above).

◄ This closet system features a unit that answers the question, "What to do with the corners?" The unit allows for open storage on the shelves and a novel closed storage space with frosted, curved doors. Any way you look at it, it's a stylish addition to a storage solution.

■ Small shelves, racks, and cabinets with transparent doors solve the storage problem of an individual who has a little bit of everything. This solution is especially useful in rooms without space for a dresser or a chest. It also provides instant visibility, as well as letting you grab what you need without hesitation or rummaging through the contents of a drawer.

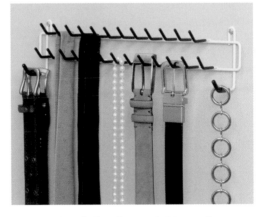

▲ If you take a look at the way clothing retailers store their ties, you'll usually find them flat. That's because ties are woven on the bias, and flat storage helps keep them straight. Flat storage (in shallow drawers) is going to be at a premium at home, however. Instead, hanging racks help keep them neat and out of the way. Both of the racks shown here accommodate belts too.

Furniture

Chests of drawers, trunks, dressers, drawer units, nightstands, armoires—the list of furniture you can use for bedroom storage is virtually limitless. Any piece of furniture with open space will add to the style of your room and increase its storage potential—even tables, whose open space underneath you can conceal with skirting.

When choosing furniture for bedroom storage, appearance is equally important as storage potential. If you pick furniture at random, with no attention to consistency of style, you may get more storage, but your bedroom can look like a stylistic circus—not a quality conducive to creating a place of respite.

Approach your freestanding furniture as a system in itself, making decisions about what kind of item is best contained by what enclosure. For example, in the summer, heavy sweaters can go in the drawers or in a cedar chest at the foot of the bed. Move them to shelves in the winter so you can get at them easily. Keep socks and other small items separated with drawer dividers.

▲ Some form of nightstand or night table is almost essential to every bedroom. The top provides a place for lamps, the alarm clock, and other pieces you want on display. A nightstand with a drawer is perfect for corralling your collection of bedtime reading material.

► A modular furniture system can be configured to fit a variety of storage needs. An entertainment system, books, or display items are all welcome in this contemporary design.

► Even a small armoire can offer a multitude of uses. Outfitted here with a sliding keyboard tray, it functions as a small hideaway office or study center. It has plenty of room below for books and files. Other configurations make it the perfect enclosure for your television and sound system.

▲ The foot of the bed is often an area with excess available space—just the right spot for a low chest, cedar or otherwise, or an antique steamer trunk. If your bedroom style tends toward the avant garde, you could even use a large commercial tool box. Always consider your overall design scheme when making furniture choices. This chest, finished in solid oak, has a classic look (with false drawer fronts) but is lined with cedar, a wood whose grain and knot pattern may not fit other design themes.

► Under the bed—who would have thought of it? Although this space is oft forgotten, with the right kind of bed construction, it's perfect for low-slung storage. Use it for bed linens, extra guest towels (if the bath is nearby), or toys. The bed shown here is a commercial unit with the storage box built in, but you can make your own "box" with handles and wheels. Beds on metal frames supported by central legs may limit you to plastic boxes, but some come outfitted with wheels.

Children's rooms

There are some times when children's rooms have to be "captured" and returned to their original state. The amount of chaos a small child can create with just a few things is mindboggling. If you find that part of your yearly routine includes attacking the floor of your child's room with a shovel, it's time to reevaluate the situation.

Solving the children's room storage puzzle may prove more difficult than other spaces because of the volume of stuff stored there. If getting all of it out of the room so you can assess the situation becomes too difficult, at least get sections of it in one location—on the bed, for example. Work with your child to set up activity stations—one for reading, one for toys, one for creating things, one for games, and depending on the age of the child, another for computer activities. The same rule applies here as for adult storage—get the items used as close as possible to their respective station.

Your problem may be compounded by the fact that next month (or next week) your child may want to change the layout of the room. That's one reason kid space needs to be flexible. Modular storage units—cubes, boxes, or anything you can move around—can help here. So can a variety of strategically spaced shelving units, either freestanding (but be careful of tipping) or wall-mounted units whose purpose can be altered, if not their location.

Children's rooms should also be adaptable to changing needs with changing age. Adjustable shelving (the kind with brackets on tracks) can keep pace as the child grows up. This way the stuffed toy shelf of today can be the bookshelf of tomorrow. The small armoire with toys in it now can house the TV and CD/DVD player (the combo unit saves space) in just a few years.

◄ Chests of drawers in children's rooms can be used for clothes storage, laid out with the same principles used for adults, and for toys. Just don't get the two mixed together. A child's unit needs to be sturdy to stand up to the heavy use it will receive. A chest at the foot of the bed can store an extra blanket and double as a play table.

► Whether it is the bedroom or a bathroom, be sure to plan the kid's storage so they can easily and safely get to the things they need. If they need a boost, get a solid stool with rubber feet so it doesn't slide around.

◄ Pegs (which are nothing more than a breed of hook) come in handy in a child's room. All manner of things will get hung on them. Be sure to locate pegs at a height your child can reach.

► If your living room or other first-floor space functions as a secondary play area, a child will tend to leave these first-floor toys strewn around when playtime is over. Rather than fight this tendency, you can go with it and put a toy-storage box in the living room—until he or she grows up and out of it. If the colorful model shown here doesn't fit the decor of your living space, put this one in the child's room and use a more traditional storage chest or trunk—something with a lid light enough for the child to lift when retrieving toys (and putting them back, of course). Better yet, install lid supports, the kind that hold the lid in position when opened. That way it won't slam down on a child's fingers.

Tips for kid's-room storage

A child's room has most of the same storage opportunities as an adult room. You just need to find them.

■ Look up and under. Use the space above windows for shelving that shows off trophies, collections, artwork, and things that are expressions of a child's personality or achievement. Be wary of such locations above doors, however. Each closing of the door can move the objects ever so slightly until they fall off. Creating under the bed storage is easy. Either make rolling bins (with dividers) or purchase see-through plastic tubs on wheels. Or you can buy the solution ready made—bed and storage drawer in one unit. The space under the bed is also a good location for a trundle—an extra bed that doesn't interfere with the rest of the room and can be pulled out for sleepovers.

■ Bookshelves are an effective means of getting items off the floor, but they can become remarkably cluttered. Use bins and storage containers instead.

■ Keep games and their pieces in plastic storage boxes on lower shelves in a game center.

■ Invest in an armoire. Without getting any larger, it can grow as your child does. It's just right with a rod or a shelf at eye level for baby's clothes. Later you might want to add cubbies to both the top and bottom sections to keep toys and playthings organized. After a few years, and with a little modification, it becomes the perfect entertainment center.

■ Find a photo center—a place for photo albums, scrapbooks, loose pictures (because everything won't make it into a scrapbook or album), saved schoolwork, and other memorabilia. This doesn't have to be located in the child's room, but you should have a file cabinet or drawer of some kind so you can safely tuck this stuff away.

◄ As children grow, their needs for storage will change. By mid-teens, the toy box will have disappeared, replaced by closed and open storage solutions that reflect your children's personalities and ongoing involvement with school and studies.

◄ Make media portable with a teen-size rolling table large enough to accommodate a television, CD/DVD player, and one or two other electronic items. The two drawers along the bottom keep CDs and games from taking flight and landing in various spots in the room. This mobile media stand could just as well function as a craft table that could be pushed against the wall when not in use. Scissors, tape, and supplies go in the drawers below.

3

BEDROOMS

■ Closet systems are for little people too—actually for any age. That's the beauty of adjustable systems. They are the definition of adaptability. Set up the system when the child is young and as he or she grows, keep raising the bar—the one for clothes, that is. You may need to make the system wider or bring it around the corner of a closet as the child grows up, but these are inexpensive and easy to implement changes.

► Here's an example of efficient use of space: Rather than end the bunk-bed frame with slats or panels, this unit comes outfitted with a computer workspace, complete with a pullout tray for the keyboard. You can incorporate the same idea into existing furnishings. Pullout keyboard trays are available for such retrofit installations.

◄ Cap off your design with color coordination. The use of color shown here, in the door panels, bed frame, desktop, and some of the items on display helps unify the design scheme. Such unity brings order to the room and contributes to the tranquil atmosphere. A room that looks intentionally attractive tends to be kept that way.

Bathrooms

Getting yourself from a disorderly bathroom to one that's neat and functional is a process that uses the same techniques as in other cluttered rooms—pull everything out and put it back in a commonsense place. "Everything" means the soap, toothpaste, toothbrushes, and the deodorant. The major difference with bathroom stuff is that it tends to be smaller. You should still be able to tackle an average bath in a couple of hours. Better get the bathroom out of the way all at once—otherwise you'll be tempted to put everything back in a jumble.

Sorting out a bathroom is also easier in one respect: It's not likely you'll have items to put in a "for sale" or "storage" box. Bathroom items fall into one of two categories. They are either essential or candidates for a heave-ho. This includes half-used shampoos and soaps you no longer like and the free-sample collection that keeps falling off the shelf when you open the medicine cabinet. Frayed towels and washcloths with holes or stains go in the rag drawer. Get them there, but don't stop to cut them up right now. You might lose your sorting momentum. If there are things you don't really need, but can't part with, cart

Chapter 4 highlights

STORAGE LAYOUTS
Where you put the storage relative to where you use it is one of the challenges associated with creating good storage.

54

TOWELS AND LINENS
Towels and linens are more than a storage item. They become part of a room's decor.

56

TOILETRIES AND MEDICINES
These are the necessities that clutter up a bathroom quickest. Move them off the countertop yet keep them within easy reach.

62

STAYING ORGANIZED
Getting organized is, in many ways, easier than staying the course. But with good storage solutions, the job becomes easier.

66

FUNCTIONAL DISPLAY
Making a room attractive is part of the job of an effective storage solution.

67

them off to some remote location—preferably the trash bin, but at least to a shelf in the basement or garage.

One other thing you should do in a bathroom reordering that might not apply to other rooms (except perhaps the kitchen)— wipe everything clean before restoring order. Bathroom items, no matter how efficient your exhaust fan, tend to pick up soap film, which tends to pick up dust. Once you get everything off the shelves, wipe the shelves clean. Then do the same for each item as you put it back. Bathrooms should be like a bedroom with water—a place of privacy, one that feels restful—at least at the end of the day. In the morning its role may be reversed, as family members stream in and out in hurried preparation for the day. Both roles are better served by an uncluttered environment.

Storage layouts

▶ A large walk-in closet just off the bathroom makes dressing easy. More shelving on the wall would add extra storage. Master baths are often a series of smaller rooms connected as a private suite.

Layout and lifestyle go hand in hand, and nowhere is this more true than in planning storage solutions. Bathroom organization for two adults without children looks much different than for a family with kids.

You'll want to use every inch of storage space in your bathroom, and you can do that either by remodeling the existing space or relying on accessories if a renovation isn't in the budget. Consider accessories that keep your bathroom organized and minimize stooping, bending over, and reaching.

Design is most effective when it leaves the room uncluttered and helps provide a sense of order. Linen and storage closets in a bathroom keep towels and supplies available but hidden so you can display only those elements that add definition and focus to your bathroom. Closet doors also add architectural detail to the space. Built-in storage in or near a bathroom area can also serve as organized closet space for clothing and shoes.

Here are a few storage solutions you can consider—either as independent add-ons or as part of a renovation plan:
- Furniture-style vanities
- Medicine cabinets
- Drawers with storage dividers
- Linen closets
- Open shelving (great for towels, soaps, and decorative items)
- A tall, narrow cabinet near toilet for scrub brushes and cleaners
- Built-in niche in closet for laundry baskets
- Enclosed storage for kids' needs (supplies and bath toys)
- Rolling/mobile shelves or storage units
- Towel bars, hooks, and racks
- Hand-towel rings
- Freestanding furniture
- Revolving trays in cabinets
- Built-in ironing board

◀ Two sinks and an abundance of storage allow multiple family members to use the space. Adequate storage keeps bathroom clutter to a minimum.

▶ Bright but easy on the eye, the dressing area of this children's bath is perfect for a youngster. As children grow older, change color schemes and accents to accommodate changing tastes.

Developing bathroom style

Many people tend to think of style as it refers to popular decorating themes, such as country, Tuscan, Asian, traditional, French provincial, or contemporary. "Style" also defines a group of concepts that affect the look and feel of a room. Use these tools—color, texture, shape, line, and form—when planning the bathroom of your dreams. Notice how each of the arrangements photographed create pleasing, but entirely different, effects. Strong colors and textures dominate the scene on the near right. Subtle colors set the tone on the far right. Neither is more correct than the other. What matters is what's pleasing for you.

Towels and linens

Planning storage for towels and linens is a lot like following the watchword of real estate—it's all about "location, location, location." What you have to consider for towels is three locations—one where you need to use them, one where you need to put them while they're waiting to be used, and one where you'll toss them when they're ready for the wash.

At a minimum you need at least one implement—a hook, ring, or towel bar handy to the shower or tub. The same goes for vanities—one hook on one side of a single sink cabinet and on both sides of a double vanity. If your space prohibits even this single fixture, put the towels and washcloths in a basket or small wheeled container, anything you can move back and forth when you need it.

Fresh towels can go almost anywhere you have space—on towel bars, shelves, hooks, racks, or in cabinets. Closed storage units create a clean uncluttered look, something that might be important in small spaces. Open storage puts towels (and everything else) on display. The items themselves must be stored neatly to avoid looking disorganized.

When they're ready for the wash, towels can go into hampers, baskets, or under-the-vanity pullout containers. Just make sure the container allows enough air circulation to let moisture evaporate.

► Here's an "industrial" solution that doesn't come off heavy-handed. Sturdy baker's racks (available at home centers and bath specialty shops) provide plenty of additional storage space for towels. The racks won't set you back a fortune and assemble quickly. What keeps this heavy-framed solution from looking monstrous is the narrow width of the unit and the proportion of its height to its width. A different configuration might work just fine in a larger bathroom, but this one fits nicely on a narrow wall. These towels could just as well have been stored in a cabinet or closet, but this rack puts them right where they're needed—next to the shower.

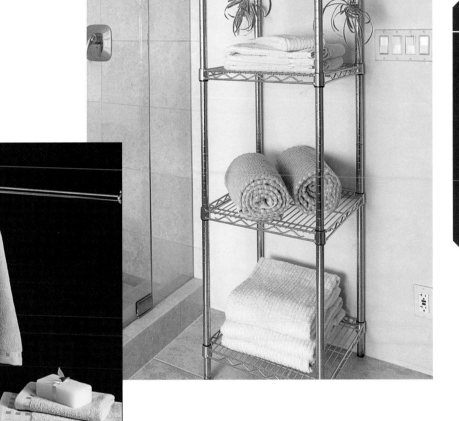

◄ An additional towel bar and small antique side table provide an add-on solution when you need more towel storage in a room that won't allow renovation. This is just enough storage space for the additional towels. A larger table or closed cabinet might have overwhelmed the space and created a feeling of confinement.

◀ Small things create big solutions. When you don't have room for cabinets and even wall shelving would get in the way, think small. This wicker case, purchased unfinished and painted white to match the overall decor, adds just enough towel storage in this tiny bath.

4

BATHROOMS

💡 GOOD IDEA

EASY STORAGE OPTIONS

■ If you can't build in a linen closet, opt for a freestanding closed-storage unit. There are plenty of styles to be found at your home center and bathroom design shop.

■ Baskets—in all sizes, shapes, and colors—are the universal storage solution when you've run out of options. You can stack them on the floor or just use a large basket for towels. Move it close to the shower to put dry towels within reach, then back against the wall when you're done.

▶ Narrow thinking can create the perfect solution to bathroom towel storage. Adding a freestanding linen tower increases the open storage space on a narrow wall. It also provides an attractive stylistic element in the design scheme. Freestanding furniture provides a more immediate, less costly, and better looking solution than trying to figure out how to add built-in closets.

▼ A narrow glass shelf over a sink or next to the toilet provides an attractive towel rack without taking up floor or closet space.

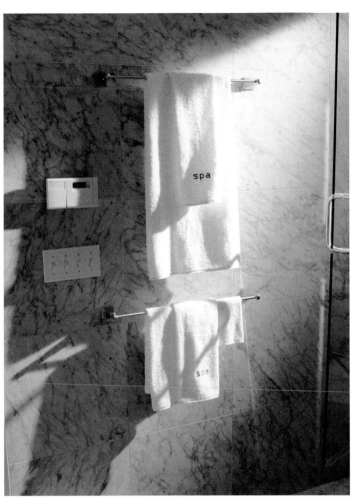

■ Open towel storage is something a bathroom can't get enough of. Adding more hooks, bars, and rings for towels and washcloths is almost always a good idea, as long as the location is functional. You may need to get the towels close to the shower—that calls for a proximate location. If you just need more storage space, choose a location that displays your towels but doesn't get in the way. Notice also that the towels themselves become design elements in their own right. So does the arrangement of accessories like the contrasting small boxes (opposite) on the glass shelf. Choose colors and textures to complement your overall design scheme.

▲ Even when you have plenty of closed storage space for towels and linens, you'll want some close by the "stations" where you'll need to use them—on one side (or both) of the vanity and within reach of the tub or shower. You'll also need a transition spot for towels on their way to the laundry. Almost anything will do, such as the small stool to the right of the vanity, or a hamper. Just make sure your "outgoing" space doesn't fill up or spill over.

◀ Freestanding furniture can add style and storage space to your bathroom at the same time. This double hutch could be outfitted with wood panels that would hide the contents, but the glass fronts keep the size of the structure from overwhelming the space.

 GOOD IDEA

BEHIND THE DOOR
If you've exhausted all your options for creating additional towel storage, look to the back of the bathroom door—a good place for a row of hooks or a commercial hanging rack. Some even feature fold-out bars for added convenience. Once you've moved the raggedy towels to the rag bin, organize what's left into sets, to keep your use of them looking orderly.

► The same retrofit wire-basket solution found in updated kitchens can be applied to your bathroom too. Here the basket is mounted on glides in the vanity cabinet, providing an easily accessible solution for towels that are ready for the wash. The basket—or any dirty-towel container in the bathroom—also saves time. Grabbing an armful of towels all at once takes less effort than running one or two at a time to the laundry.

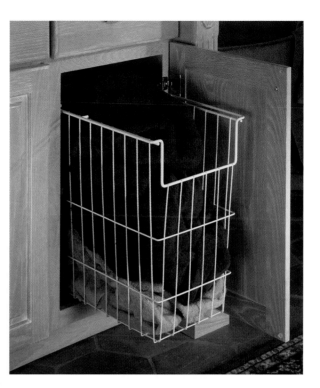

▲ Make stylistic decisions at the same time you're increasing your storage space. There are very few bathrooms in which this tower cabinet wouldn't look at home. When you shop for such items, give your imagination a little running room—this idea could be mimicked with an antique if it complements your design scheme.

▲ Don't have room for a linen closet? Maybe you do and don't know it. If you have a closet in the next room that's deeper than you need, borrow a couple of feet and use it to create closet space in the bathroom. A recessed linen closet like this doesn't eat up space by extending into the room.

Toiletries and medicines

Small things go in small spaces—that's the rule of thumb for storing toiletries and medicines. Narrow shelves, small bins, and other diminutive spots won't hold larger items such as towels. Reserve these areas for the jars, bottles, containers, and "equipment" associated with getting ready in the morning.

Weed through (and weed out) your collection before re-storing them. Toss expired medicines and old makeup. The medicines can be harmful if used, and old makeups can harbor bacteria. Consolidate shampoo samples into one container, or better yet, throw them out too. Apparently none of the samples have become a favorite of yours, or it wouldn't still be there. Then while you've got your momentum up, tackle the cleaning agents. You probably only need one or two—an all-purpose spray and a nonabrasive compound. Two sponges at the

most should get you by. All of this stuff, along with a pair of rubber gloves and a cleaning rag for quick wipe-ups, can go under the vanity sink. Keep cleaning stuff separate from paper goods and personal care items by using baskets or bins. Plastic boxes are good organizers, too, and wiping them clean is a snap.

Extend your urge to organize to your vanity drawers and medicine cabinet. Get wooden dividers or shallow metal or plastic baskets to keep makeup and toiletries from becoming a homogenized pile. Use small cups or plastic glasses to store makeup brushes and lipstick pencils. And for a really modern (maybe even mechanically chic) retrofit, get a toolbox with drawers. Home centers and hardware stores carry a variety of these items—they're perfect for storing lots of little stuff.

◄ Deep open shelves are a great place to store numerous items, but their depth can prove inconvenient for items you need to use daily. Reserve these shelves for things that need only occasional use.

► The space between studs (especially those on 24-inch centers) harbors a wonderful potential for recessed storage areas, both closed and open. You can cut away the drywall and mount a prefab cabinet, or frame in one to your own dimensions. Such storage units, though not very deep from front to back, are perfect for items that don't need a lot of room, such as toiletries and medicines. Whether prefab or crafted at home, adjustable shelves are a must—to accommodate items of different heights. Use organizers to keep small things readily available.

Making your bathroom kid-safe

In children's bathrooms, parents must pay special attention to safety, durability, and adaptability.

- Use slip-resistant materials on floors and bathtubs.
- Avoid multiple levels in a bath or steps to the tub.
- Use only those receptacles, lights, and switches that are protected with ground fault circuit interrupters (GFCIs).
- Include a seat or bench in a shower.
- Use night-lights to illuminate the hallway and the bathroom.
- Install privacy locks that you can easily open in the event of an emergency.
- Use soap dispensers in the shower.
- Install outlet safety covers.
- Install childproof latches and locks on cabinet and vanity doors and drawers.
- Install safety covers over sharp vanity/countertop corners, the tub spout, and other sharp areas.
- Install towel hooks at "kid height."
- Use only unbreakable drinking glasses in the bath area.
- Have a child-safe step stool nearby or install a built-in step by the sink.
- Check your water heater and set it to no higher than 120°F.
- Install a tub and shower temperature regulator to prevent scalding.
- Don't install heated towel bars in baths used by small children.

- Never leave young children unattended in the bathroom; small amounts of standing water and toilets present drowning hazards. Install toilet lid locks if you have toddlers in the house.
- Keep medicines and cleaning supplies out of the reach of children.

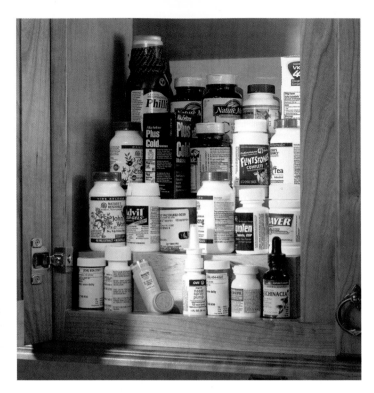

◄ Stair-stepped storage in a medicine cabinet makes good use of the front-to-back area. It keeps medicines organized, visible, and easy to retrieve.

▼ When you need storage for shampoos and soaps, nothing beats cubbies in the shower wall. The recesses put the items right where you need them—no transporting them back and forth between the shower and a shelf elsewhere in the room. Cubbies are difficult to seal in retrofit installations, but are an excellent addition to renovated shower space.

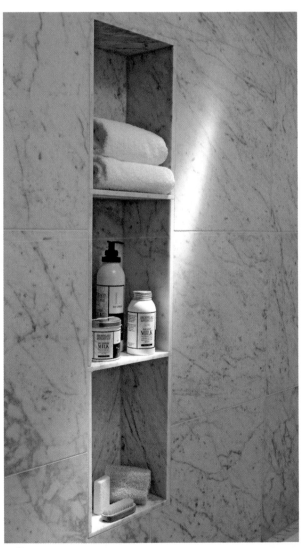

◄ A wicker shelf like this can be a real find when you're out browsing for storage additions to your home. It combines both open and closed spaces, which adds versatility to its handsome design.

► An accessory shelf (many styles are available) can create a place for daily use items when you don't have room for a larger cabinet.

◄ Large, open storage can be the place for things that are left after you've sorted through your bathroom stuff and put the frequently used items in areas within reach of the vanity. Storage space for such items can be located down the hall and still be considered close enough to be convenient.

▲ Ceramic trays and shelves can be easily retrofitted into an existing shower. Most mount on brackets affixed to the wall. Drilling the tile for the bracket fasteners is easy to do with a masonry drill bit.

Staying organized

Good storage should not be something you achieve on a once-a-year basis. It's a habit, and making the right decisions about where things go in your bathroom will help you keep them organized. One organized location, such as wire baskets in the vanity drawers, will spawn another. You'll want the same order and experience the same convenience with all of your things.

The place to start is your vanity—the primary vehicle for bathroom storage. It should be clear by now that it's not merely housing for the sink, or a repository of "homeless" items. To start with, a two-doored vanity without shelves or drawers probably won't do. If you can replace it, look for units that resemble furniture or at least include drawers and shelves. You can even retrofit your existing vanity if you need to keep it: Tack wire racks on the inside of the doors, install pullout or stationary shelves or drawers on glides or 1× rails, and fasten towel hooks or racks to the sides. You'll find inexpensive fixtures in durable, tasteful styles at your home center or department store.

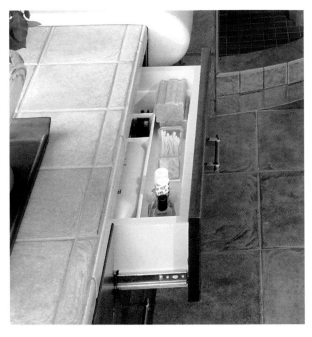

▲ Primary storage in a bathroom comes from base cabinets, which offer many options, including doors, drawers, and slide-out trays.

▲ Well planned storage makes your countertops available for decorative accents rather than cosmetic clutter. Put the most frequently used items, such as toothpaste and lotion, in the top drawer near the sink. Dividers or baskets in drawers aid organization of toiletries.

▲ A pullout or built-in laundry hamper makes laundry storage handy. You can put a pullout in the vanity or reduce the width of the drawers in an existing built-in cabinet, reframe them, and install a built-in hamper in the empty space.

Functional display

Towels, soap, and toiletries may be primarily functional items, but they also have strong design appeal. Take full advantage of the possibilities by artfully displaying them on towel racks, open shelving, built-in niches, or in baskets by the bath or shower.

▲ A woven basket holds soap and towels.

▲ Open shelving provides the best place to show things off. If you have the space, you can use a spot like this to help establish the mood of the room, without including functional items. The legitimate function of this space then becomes purely aesthetic.

◄ A family photograph, a shaving brush, and clear canisters filled with toiletries work easily together.

Kitchens

No room has more storage issues than the kitchen. Not only must most kitchens store food, prep tools, and serveware, the kitchen also multitasks as foyer, mudroom, communications center, study center, office, studio, and dining room. Cabinets, drawers, and countertops break space into chunks that help keep things in their place, but kitchens that make life simpler go even further.

Do you know where your fire extinguisher is? How about the almond extract? How much time do you spend looking for items your family can't find? Do hobby supplies always sit on the table waiting for a lift to their proper place?

Imagine a kitchen in which tools nearly leap into your hands, they're just as easy to put away, and you can find your cheesecake pan when you need it. Use the ideas on these pages to make your kitchen work for you.

Taking stock of storage

What's the biggest obstacle in your kitchen? Taking too many

Chapter 5 highlights

POTS, PANS, TOOLS, AND TRAYS
These are the mainstays of meal preparation. You want them where they are easy to reach.

70

STORING APPLIANCES
Where do you put the workhorses of kitchen clatter? Somewhere out of sight, but not out of easy reach.

74

DISHES AND GLASSWARE
You need them in a flash and when they're stored you have to keep them from breaking.

76

FOOD STORAGE
Food storage is a special art in itself. Fortunately many tools are available to minimize hassles and waste.

78

SHELVES FOR SHOWING OFF
Ambience is as important in the kitchen as anywhere else, and attractive items displayed on shelves help create enjoyable space.

82

TOWELS AND CLEANING SUPPLIES
The bane of kitchen storage, nothing seems to work to keep them accessible yet out of the way.

86

steps to find and put away your cutting boards, knives, and mixing bowls? Or pawing through a base cabinet to find your watering can and houseplant food? Start on one section or issue, but mull others as you go. As you fine-tune your storage, extra space will appear in other cabinets. Keep these tips in mind as you plot the perfect kitchen storage:

Break the rules. Just because dishes are typically stored in upper cabinets doesn't mean you have to store them there.

Keep safety close. Store the fire extinguisher in an accessible place, near the stove. Really.

Stash stuff where it's used. This goes for non-kitchen stuff too. If the kids draw every day at the kitchen table, store their crayons and paper in a basket or drawer near the table.

Divide and conquer. Group like items (on shelves, in tubs, in baskets) and you'll find them faster than rummaging through a cabinet full of items.

Pots, pans, tools, and trays

Pots and pans can plague you with storage problems because no two have exactly the same use, size, or shape. If you have a pot-storage problem, that's exactly where you should begin—sort them first by use, then by size and shape. Start with the big stuff—stockpots and pasta cookers—and work your way down. Saucepans go together and so do frying pans and saute pans. Then collect all the baking pans in one spot. Get everything out of the drawers and cupboards and put the groupings on the countertop (this not only helps you sort the stuff, it opens up space you'll use when you put them back).

Now assess your space and put the pots close to where you use them. Deep drawers near the cooking center are good for oversize pots. So is a large base cabinet with heavy-duty pullouts. Stack the baking pans inside each other and put them near the oven. Even IN the oven is better than across the room. You don't have to put the lids on the pots. They're better off in a shallow drawer (install vertical pegs to separate them), or for easy access, slide them into vertical dividers (you can build one to fit under the cabinet if you have enough countertop space).

▲ Nothing gets cooking pots closer to where you'll use them than a suspended pot rack. Pick a style from a multitude of manufacturers—there's something for everyone—and hang it yourself. Get the rack high enough to keep cooking grease from accumulating on the pots, but low enough for the cook to easily disengage them.

▲ Fully extendable pullout shelves in the base cabinets eliminate the struggle to access items stored at the back. These full-extension slides are designed to withstand heavy use.

▲ Open shelves benefit from pullouts too. Line a shelf with baskets and you've put together a pullout system, minus the glides. Many homeowners choose this option for the visual interest that baskets add to the kitchen. Tip: If the finish on your shelves tends to get sticky, line the shelf with clear or patterned shelf paper.

▲ Drawers are easy—with no door to open before reaching a shelf, drawers offer one-move access. Here deep, broad drawers on heavy-duty glides are an ideal place to stash large pots.

▲ Tambours are not just for hiding appliances. They put shallow pots and pans—or your lid collection—within easy reach.

▶ Tall, vertical racks are large enough to store sizable dishes, cookie sheets, and trays. They make good spots for keeping cookbooks too.

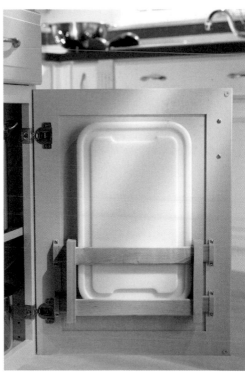

▲ If you're short on open space in which to house vertical dividers, make use of other vertical surfaces in your kitchen. Store cutting boards and other thin items in racks fastened to the inside of your cabinet doors.

▲ Pots, pans, and lids are awkward to stack, store, and access on deep, fixed base cabinet shelves. Not so when the shelves are pullout wire racks.

5

KITCHENS

■ Cutlery dividers keep eating utensils separated. Make your own or install a commercial unit. Even plastic compartments are better than a drawerful of loose utensils. If you keep carving knives in drawers, use a knife holder, or on a countertop, use a slotted wood knife block. Or line your drawers with cork or spongy shelf liner in a range of colors and patterns and your knives (or utensils) will stay put every time you open and close the drawer.

▲ Swing-out shelves hinged to cabinet stiles create easily accessible space. They offer the convenience of pullouts without the necessity of extending a rolling tray to its full length.

▲ This combination pullout cutting and preparation center keeps cutting implements close to where you'll need them and frees up countertop space for other storage needs.

▶ It's wise to design a kitchen to minimize unnecessary actions, such as bending over, stooping, reaching deep into cupboards, and lifting heavy appliances and dishes. Pullouts and swing-outs reduce unnecessary movement and save your energy for the real thing—cooking to your heart's content.

▶ Using the toe-kick space under cabinets puts every available inch of cabinets to work. They're ideal for flat objects that see only occasional use, such as large serving trays.

Corner treatments

Kitchen corners can appear to pose difficult design and storage problems. What to do with them? They seem to be perfect opportunities for wasted space and family traffic jams. But with the right storage implements—in this case a variety of lazy Susan designs—they become a functioning aspect of your kitchen you can't get along without.

Many manufacturers make the traditional two-tray lazy Susan with bifold doors, but other styles are available. You'll find some units made with independently revolving trays. These units feature single-door access, which is much more convenient. They are designed to present a 45-degree surface across the front of the corner, not the conventional right-angle solution. (That makes the back of the countertop corner easier to get to and more useable.)

Other designs combine the revolving tray with pie-shaped wire pullouts or plastic trays with individual pullout sections.

5

KITCHENS

Storing appliances

Whether you store your small appliances behind some kind of closed door or leave them out in open storage rests largely on personal taste and convenience. If you like the way your appliances look out in the open, and find them more accessible that way, then so be it. What matters is accessibility.

In the case of small appliances, accessibility should include not just getting to your kitchen machines but also having enough room to use them comfortably. If you can't pour the ground coffee from the coffee mill directly into the coffee basket without moving everything around, you probably should reassess their placement. Make sure all the related "support" products are close to the place of business—coffee and sugar for the brewer, flour and salt for the mixer, bread for the toaster.

If closed storage strikes you as preferable, you can hide your machines behind cupboard doors or the ever-popular tambour doors of an appliance garage. If you go the garage route, keep the area in front of it clear. The appliances in the garage "own" the space in front of it also.

If there's any single "rule" governing appliance storage, it's this—keep frequently used machines at or below eye level. Storing them above your reach is dangerous (and inefficient). Slow cookers, deep fryers, and electric roasters should probably go in the base cabinets outfitted with lazy Susans or swing-out shelves.

■ Appliance garages with tambour doors are the traditional storage structure for small appliances. They provide a neat, orderly, and accessible way to hide frequently used appliances. If you're planning a renovation that includes an appliance garage, make sure its "roof" will be high enough to accommodate the tallest piece of machinery that goes in it.

■ Small appliances can vie with your food preparation activities for the space under your wall cabinets. You can remove this struggle for priority by housing some small appliances in their own undercabinet shelving. Your multispeed mixer or blender might be too tall for such a shelf, but a small microwave will fit nicely. Make sure the unit is properly vented to dissipate the heat.

◄ Corners are great locations for appliance garages. By extending the wall cabinets down to the countertop and installing a door, you create a diagonal space that's just the right size for a toaster garage without cramping your counter space. (Countertop corners are often too deep, anyway, to be practical for food preparation.) Here you've solved a design and storage problem with one stroke.

◄ Storing appliances next to or near their areas of use saves steps and energy. For example, with the mixer next door, and the mixing bowls below, you can set up this pullout mixing station in a moment's notice.

CLOSER LOOK

THE VERSATILITY OF PULLOUTS

Deep spaces can hold lots of stuff, but on fixed shelves your things—particularly those stashed in the back—can be tough to access. So put in a pullout. A gentle pull brings what's deep in the back to light, right in front of you. With pullouts, difficult spaces become more versatile, and your ability to store what you want where you want it increases.

Pullouts needn't require a new or remodeled kitchen. At its most basic, a basket or tub on a shelf is a pullout. For existing cabinets, manufacturers now offer vast collections of wood and wire pullout storage products that are easy to install. These products come in a range of sizes and are sold at hardware stores and home centers. If you like, you can even make—or have someone make for you—pullout shelves to your own specifications, and paint or stain them to complement your décor. If you are building or remodeling your kitchen, be sure to explore the many options of pullout features available in new cabinetry.

Smart kitchen design

Whether you organize your kitchen according to the principles of the work triangle or activity centers, your kitchen storage plans should be based upon common sense.

- Keep food and other often used items as close as possible to the relevant appliance or area where you will use them.
- Store food in cabinets attached to cool outside walls or near shaded windows.
- Avoid placing cabinets near the dishwasher, oven, refrigerator, and warm exterior walls.
- Spices and cooking oils should be within easy reach of the cooktop.
- Store frequently used items within easy reach. Store less-used ones in the back of a cabinet or up high.
- Having a section of countertop lower than the rest is helpful for chopping and other prep work, and it also gives the kids an easy place to prepare a quick snack.
- An island equipped with a sink combines effective storage with food preparation.

5

KITCHENS

Dishes and glassware

Dishes and glassware intended for daily use should be stored near the dishwasher or sink. This lets you dispose of food scraps and clean them easily. Ideally you should locate this storage area close to the food preparation area, which allows you to load up serving dishes easily. Your formal dinnerware should be stored near the dining table.

Whether you use closed or open storage is a matter of personal choice. If your dishware is colorful or otherwise attractive, you might opt for vertical storage dividers and open shelving. Store infrequently used glasses and cups behind closed doors (consider doors with glass panels to add an element of display) and upside down if you want to keep them dust free. Stemware stores easily on a hanging rack mounted under the cabinets (make sure they don't interfere with preparation space) or under a cabinet shelf.

■ Vertical racks make colorful plates part of your kitchen decorating scheme. Locate daily dishes next to the sink or dishwasher for easy cleanup.

▼ Many pullout trays—if pulled out too fast—will cause stacked dishes to fall toward the back of the cabinet—not something you want to contend with when preparing even a routine meal. High-back pullouts keep stacked dishes from suffering this fate.

▲ Manufacturers now offer drawers with slot-secured dividers such as those shown here, as well as vertical pegs suited for dividing stacks of plates and bowls. Dishes are less likely to break when they're stored lower to ground level.

▲ Pots, pans, and lids in drawers deep enough to store them can make them difficult to get to and prone to breakage if you close the drawer too quickly. This pullout tray, equipped with wire racks, keeps access easy and reduces breakage by keeping the surfaces from touching.

▲ There's no rule that says a cabinet door has to swing open on side-mounted hinges. Installing an under-the-cabinet unit and outfitting it with a top-hinged door leaves dishes at an easy-to-retrieve shoulder height.

▶ The strongest part of stemware is the stem itself. Sliding it into slots on a hanging shelf, ether mounted on the wall or under the cabinet, makes the best use of otherwise dead space.

GOOD IDEA

STORE WITHIN REACH
Helping with kitchen chores, such as setting the table and unloading the dishwasher, is easier for young children when the goods are within their limited reach. Store flatware and table-setting gear near the table (or out of the cook's work area). Store dishes and cups on low shelves in a base cabinet near the dishwasher. When your helpers are quite small and just getting the hang of handling dishes, consider swapping your ceramics for a good-looking set of durable plastic dishes.

Food storage

Food pantries make good meals. A well-organized pantry system makes it easy for you to see at a glance the ingredients you have on hand. Some kitchens have a space that effectively stores all the foodstuff, in others you'll need to install more than one food center.

Whatever food storage solutions you rely on, access is the key (after avoiding contamination and spoilage, of course). Here's where slide-outs and pullouts really get their chance to shine. They make access convenient and keep items visible so you remember to use them before their expiration date forces you to throw them out. Here are some general tips for storing food.

Canned foods don't last forever. Toss anything more than two years old. What you keep, store in a cool place.

Staples, such as flour and sugar, need to be kept clean, dry, and bug free. Plastic containers with snap-on lids make the best storage for these foods.

Herbs won't last more than a few months out in the open. You can extend their longevity by storing them in the freezer.

Bulk items can devour storage space. Divide their contents to make them easier to store. Put them in plastic containers with lids and label them—what kind of food it is and the recommended expiration date. Pull foods purchased earlier to the front, put later purchases toward the back.

Vegetables, such as potatoes and onions, will keep a long time in drawers that provide good air circulation.

▼ **Keep small packaged goods within view by hanging wire baskets and racks on a pantry door. You may have to trim the shelves so the rack won't bump into them when you close the door, but you'll gain a lot of convenience and increased visibility of what's inside.**

 GOOD IDEA

PANTRY SMARTS

Pantries can swallow (and then hide) as much stuff as they store. Size alone doesn't determine what a space can store. Help your pantry keep its contents easy to access by grouping items of like sizes together. Then turn to baskets, see-through tubs, stacking sets of small drawers, shelf risers, and lazy Susans so that your favorite spice mix doesn't slip into oblivion between the family size cans of broth and pasta sauce.

▲ **In the same space that an upper cabinet would require, this arrangement splits shelf duty between the rear wall and the door. It's a great way to store oils, spices, specialty items, and small packaged goods.**

 GOOD IDEA

REFURB YOUR BOARD

Lots of older kitchen cabinets have slots for pullout cutting boards. If your board is worn and cracked, reattach the front to a piece of melamine shelving, cut to size, and you'll have an easy to clean pullout work surface instead. The extra surface will come in handy when everyone crowds the kitchen for breakfast and lunch.

 DESIGN TIP

SHELF SAVVY

When planning broad pullout shelves for food storage, remember that you'll be storing food in shallow layers—so err on the side of having more shelves than fewer. In a base cabinet you'll be viewing most of your food from the top of its package, so you might want to store cans on their sides with labels visible, and space the shelves according to package size.

◀ This base cabinet demonstrates an arrangement that's often found in taller pantry cabinets as well. To each side of the cabinet front, narrow multitiered racks offer easy access to small, pantry goods. Behind them, pullout shelves bring layers of food stored in the deep back to the light of day.

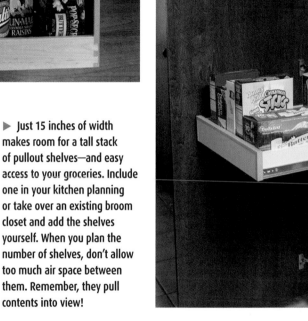

▶ Just 15 inches of width makes room for a tall stack of pullout shelves—and easy access to your groceries. Include one in your kitchen planning or take over an existing broom closet and add the shelves yourself. When you plan the number of shelves, don't allow too much air space between them. Remember, they pull contents into view!

Accessible shelving

NO MORE STEP STOOL
Hinged shelves that pull out and down from standard upper cabinets boost the accessibility of this up-high location for shorter folks.

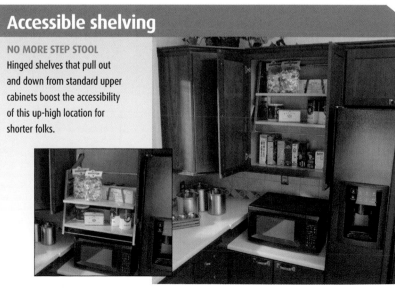

▲ Lazy Susans are traditionally located in the corners of base cabinets, but they function just as effectively in upper cabinets too.

Storing spices

▶ Splitting the storage space in a cabinet between the shelves and the door increases access to all the contents.

▶▶ This cabinet was purchased in this configuration, but you could easily modify an existing piece. Simply attach a wire or wood spice rack to the door, then shorten interior shelves to accommodate the depth of the rack. Redrill the front column of shelf-pin holes to support the shortened shelf.

▶ Cabinet options squeeze storage into a sliver's worth of space. A multitiered pullout can make a pantry in less than a 10-inch-wide space.

▼ Store on the door. Screw a door pantry on a sturdy interior door and you'll expand your kitchen's food storage capacity in minutes. The cabinet on the far right was manufactured with the door shelves in place. Check warranties before adding or modifying products.

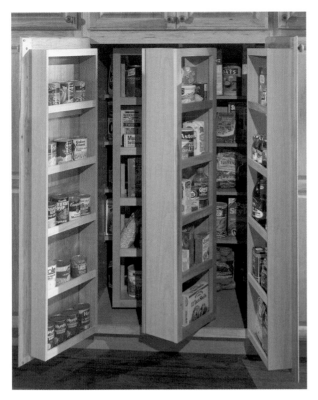

■ Pantries come in so many sizes and configurations that you're sure to find one that fits your storage needs and budget. You can even construct a pantry yourself. However you come by your pantry, consider including extra tall or wide shelves for bulky items, make as many of the shelves as adjustable as possible, and keep the shelves no deeper than 16 inches or use pullouts so the items in the back stay visible. Locate the pantry near some countertop space so you can set the grocery bags near your storage location and don't have to walk across the kitchen to put your stuff away.

Clutter cutting tips

Like any storage space, pantries get cluttered. Here are some tips on cutting the clutter. If you can, do this when you're alone—you might find the process more efficient when you can work without distraction.

■ Get everything out of the pantry and onto a countertop. Look at expiration dates and pitch anything outdated. Clean the shelves.

■ Organize your foodstuffs into primary and secondary categories. Primary stuff goes at eye level, secondary foods above and below that. Napkins, paper towels, and "support" items go on a bottom shelf. If you begin to run out of room, get the paper goods off to another location.

■ Group similar foods together— canned goods in one section (subdivided into soups, sauces, etc.), baking goods in another, pasta and rice in another.

■ While you're at it, keep lists of what you discover you need—both the grocery items you're missing and the storage containers you need.

■ Store cleaning products in a location separate from food.

Shelves for showing off

Shelves can do much more for your kitchen than provide storage space. Note how their open surfaces provide quick visibility and easy access to items you need, a strictly functional benefit. At the same time, that very visibility provides them with the potential for playing a prominent role in the design and decor of a room. Shelves, as much as any other element, can make an important contribution to the overall atmosphere of a room.

When planning shelving for your kitchen (or any room, for that matter), consider the style of the shelf itself. Plate racks with two or three grooves along their length give plates and other items a way to stand up without sliding off. Bracketed shelving brings the bracket style into the design equation. Free-hanging shelves, both with and without a back plate, seem to be suspended with no visible means of support. Rack-mounted shelves add a kind of industrial look to a wall (which you can minimize with a coat of paint).

If you think you've run out of shelf space, or wonder if your shelves secretly conspire to hide things from your view rather than show them to you, review the ideas on these pages. See something you like? Choose it for a new cabinet or modify an existing setting to yield the same function.

▲ Asymmetry can fool the eye and call attention to displayed objects, as it does here. The clock defines the "center" of the arrangement, which is balanced by the relative height consistency of the antique checkerboard and stoneware vase. The brown tones of the pieces help unify the composition and create a subtle tension with its "imbalanced" positioning.

▲ Varying the texture, shape, size, and surface materials of the objects on shelving adds to their interest. Even if they're utilitarian, the items become part of the decorative arrangement.

▶ Watered-glass door fronts add a sense of mystery to items on cabinet shelves. Glass doors combine the assets of both open and closed storage but will require more frequent cleaning, especially above a range or oven.

◀ Smooth drawer surfaces and nickel-plated pulls contrast with the textured glass and beaded board door panels.

▲ Color can make a composition playful. All of the objects on display here have a relatively consistent orange-to-red tonality. Their placement on the shelves is both practical and aesthetic. The framed picture on the left adds interest to the display, providing a contrasting shape to the round containers and plates.

 GOOD IDEA

CORRALLING YOUR CLUTTER
Forget fighting the urge to let certain things "live" on the counter or open shelving. Let them be—in a basket, maybe even several. Baskets four inches wide don't steal much counter space and can swallow daily medications and vitamins, or tea and coffee supplies. They can organize school and team notices, keys, remote controls, cell phones, and chargers. A basket is much easier to lift up for cleaning than handfuls of gathered stuff, and it's easy to swap basket size and configuration as the nature of your counter-landing stuff changes. Still feel the need for discipline? Don't allow any clutter outside of the baskets.

▲ If you like the open-shelf concept, mount rectangular display cubes in a grid—or in a stack or row—on a kitchen wall when you need just a little more storage space for dishes, cookbooks, or tools. It's an artful choice that gives a kitchen a slightly edgy look. Try black cubes on a white wall, or paint the cubes to match the wall color for a more subtle effect, as shown here.

► The arrangement of a shelved display can be critical to its visual success. Imagine these shelves with the rectangular containers on the same level. Not nearly as much interest as this diagonal placement. Imagine shelving not as individual pieces, but as a single canvas with different levels.

▼ This china hutch is actually three wall cabinets stacked on top of one another, creating a piece that is an extension of the kitchen's clean look.

► Open shelving doesn't have to "store" only utilitarian objects. This collection of stoneware dishes and vases may not see much use, but it certainly adds an artful touch to the kitchen design scheme.

▲ Shelving can create dramatic contrasts, as this black shelf on a brown-tone wall demonstrates. The effect is further intensified by the contrasting orange and yellow hues of the contents.

▲ In the dining area of this country kitchen, a galley shelf displays collectibles, drawing the eye upward. The warm wood of the crown molding, shelf, and chair rail brings unity, while the staggered heights of the objects creates variety.

▲ Even a basic concept, such as these crossed metal bands, can improve the appearance of a glass-front cabinet. In this case the style of the cabinet itself adds an accent to the style of the display.

▶ Put the corners of your cabinets to work as display spaces. This run of cabinets would not extend the full length of the wall without creating an end cabinet that would have been either too wide or too narrow. Finishing out the run with open shelving creates a nice finishing touch to the design.

Towels and cleaning supplies

Kitchen towels are not just a means of drying hands. They're a vehicle that brings color, style, softness, and personality to the kitchen—in a way that's inexpensive and easy to swap to suit whims and seasons. Who wants to hunt for a kitchen towel when you can keep them hanging and ready where you need them? Install one of these solutions in your kitchen and you won't be leaving towels on the counter or stuffing them through the fridge handle—neither of which is where you generally go to find it next time.

GOOD IDEA

GET HOOKED
Use hooks to put pot holders where you need them. It's a smart, efficient, safe solution.

GOOD IDEA

TAKE IT ELSEWHERE
In the bathroom, counter- and cabinet-mounted cup hooks can also keep hand towels and washcloths right near the sink basin.

▲ Press white plastic adhesive-backed hooks or cross-cut "hang ups" onto cabinet fronts just beneath the countertop overhang. New adhesives promise no surface damage.

▲ Screw a series of three to five small cuphooks into the underside of the countertop overhang or into the top edge of the cabinet front or side, then loop towels and potholders on the hooks. These hang between false drawer fronts, but you can mount a series at the end of an island or peninsula.

▶ Mount wooden drapery rod holders on a wall or on a base cabinet—wherever you need towel service. Drop in a drapery rod finished with decorative finials, and slip a towel loop over it. With this functional, decorative solution you can pull the towel loop forward for a clean section. When the entire loop is soiled, swap it for a fresh one. Make towel loops by machine or slip stitching together the short ends of kitchen towels. Stain or paint the drapery pieces to suit your décor, choosing a plain or decorative finial.

◀ Here are two solutions for effective storage inside a base cabinet. The first, which can be done in any existing base cabinet, is mounting a fork-like pullout hanger for dish towels. The second solution is one to consider when you are choosing new cabinets as part of a kitchen remodel. Look for a base cabinet style that maximizes available space around sink plumbing by adding a broad, low-level drawer. Store clean linens in the drawer, hang on the rod for use, and toss 'em in a basket or laundry bag when they're soiled.

 GOOD IDEA

ON THE (LOW) LEVEL
Base cabinets made with low-level drawers are suited for more than just the kitchen. Look for this feature when you're shopping for a vanity too.

Laundry solutions work in the kitchen and the garage

Unless your washer and dryer sit near the kitchen or a chute runs from the kitchen to basement laundry, where to put soiled dish cloths and towels is an issue. Here are some options, all better than crumpled, smelly heaps left on the floor, counter, or stairs waiting for a ride to the wash.

■ Set a ventilated basket under the sink. Use the basket to transport kitchen textiles to and from the laundry.

■ Stick or screw two small hooks to the inside of a base cabinet or utility closet door. Hang the corners of a small mesh lingerie bag from the hooks. (Stitch ribbon loops on the bag for hanging.) Lightweight canvas shopping totes make good laundry bags too.

■ For a bag that's more presentable, machine or slip stitch two kitchen towels into a bag. Make a drawstring casing at the top if you like.

■ In the garage, designate and label a basket, or mount hooks and a laundry bag to collect rags and towels used for yard, shop, and auto work.

▲ Whether you're planning new cabinetry or improving the function of an existing setup, there are many options for pullout recycling or trash management. The inexpensive retrofit options available at home centers, designed for one or more containers, are a smart choice even if you're installing new cabinets. Municipalities have been known to change what they'll accept for recycling; if you've installed a retrofit option, you can easily swap it for another function or scenario.

▲ Handy pullout storage to the left of the sink has a rack for dish towels and a shelf for cleaning supplies. A narrow bin keeps sponges and other items within easy reach.

▲ Do you desperately need drawers, but the space beneath your sink is all that's available? Plan a base cabinet with broad drawers anyway—then have your carpenter modify the back to fit around the sink plumbing.

▶ Snug drawers outfitted with old-fashioned pulls hold dish towels and other supplies. The drawers are within easy reach of the primary sink and the range.

5

KITCHENS

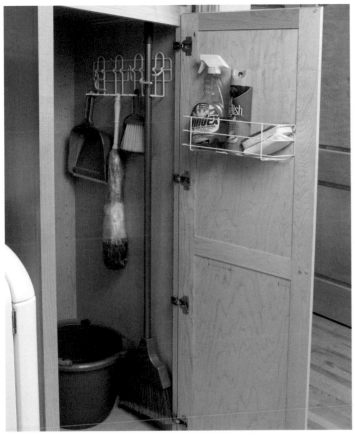

▲ Even if you feel lucky to have found space for the brooms, mops, and cleaning compounds, don't get too comfortable until you employ some device to keep them from falling all over themselves. Wooden partitions can be built into an existing utility closet. Wire racks, shelves, and handle grabbers can also be added.

▼ That same retrofit hanging shelf you've installed on another base cabinet for food storage can be put to work under the sink to house cleaning liquids.

Offices save kitchen space

Because kitchens are the hub of home activity, sometimes all chores and tasks seem to gravitate there. This puts the kitchen in the position of being grand central station—with all its attendant clutter—and maybe you just want to cook there. Having a desk area adjacent to, but not part of, the kitchen is a great design strategy for keeping clutter out of the kitchen, while making bill paying and other recordkeeping activities convenient.

Family rooms

The development of the home space known as the family room can be traced through several stages: the Victorian parlour, the library, the den, and then in the 1950s came the rec room. First it was located in the basement; it was generally a small- to medium-size space with a low ceiling and no window light. It may have held a smaller-than-regulation pool or ping-pong table, a TV, and a paperback library, and one wall might have featured a large mural depicting a natural landscape. It most certainly was finished with grooved hardboard (not hardwood) paneling. The rec room, that creation of postwar suburbia, was—for all its heralded stature and status—at best two dimensional. There was only so much you could do with its limited accommodations—even if they included a wet bar.

Today's family room, a descendant of the rec room, is anything but two dimensional. It's a multidimensional space that varies from house to house, family to family. For some it includes a library, for others one or more exercise machines. You'll find fireplaces in some family rooms, offices or hobby sectors in others,

Chapter 6 highlights

BUILT-IN STORAGE
Built-in storage is like permanent furniture. It greatly affects both the convenience and appearance of a room.

92

FREESTANDING UNITS
You can't take it with you? You can if it's freestanding storage. This kind of unit offers great flexibility when changing storage or room layouts.

96

ENTERTAINMENT CENTERS
These are the items of the present and probably the future. Make sure yours is set up for certain expansions.

98

ON DISPLAY
The atmosphere in a family room is as important as the equipment. It's the perfect place to store collections and items that provide visual interest.

101

and in almost all an entertainment center (or at least a large TV). What is common to all of them—the element that ties them together—is that the family room is instinctively the space in the house to which family members gravitate for gathering and relaxing. Because it has so many potential uses and attracts all members of the family, this room has great potential for quickly cluttering. Magazines and newspapers are often great offenders, but so are shoes, socks, toys, trinkets, snack packages, and just about anything anyone can use to leave a trail.

You can hope for the best and focus your energy on trying to get habits changed, but you've probably already tried that and know it doesn't work. The place to start is with a list of all the activities that go on in the room: reading, kid's (and pet's) play, games, TV watching, getting together with friends. Then make another list—of the things needed to support these activities. After that the question is, "Where to put them?" You'll find answers to that question on the next few pages.

Built-in storage

t's a rare room that comes perfected for storage. You have to make storage solutions. Even if you've planned and outfitted the room yourself, trends change, so do you, and so will your storage needs.

Built-in storage comes with some advantages and disadvantages. First you have to design it to meet your needs, the confines of your space, and the style of the room. You can't just go out and buy built-ins off the rack. Then you need to construct it, or hire it done. In either case the cost of a built-in storage unit will be more than preassembled storage—and if you move from your home, you can't take it with you. It's also going to be there more or less forever, so you need to design it carefully. Yet you may find these disadvantages small and the cost more than worth it.

Built-in storage can dramatically alter the appearance and style of a room, so if you're thinking about a major renovation or total makeover

use the built-in as the centerpiece of your new design. What's really appealing about built-in cabinets is that you can customize them to fit available space—especially narrow recesses in a wall. You can also use them to divide large rooms into more functional space, for example, separating the exercise equipment from the entertainment areas.

The typical style of a built-in cabinet places closed storage base cabinets on the bottom and open shelving on the top. This arrangement allows you to keep less attractive items behind closed doors and display things you like the looks of. It also allows you to restrict access to items. There is no rule, however, that restricts you to this arrangement. After all, this is your built-in. If you want closed storage on the top and open shelves on the bottom, put them there.

◀ Gone are the days of the paneled wet bar—thankfully. This modern "winged" wet bar, finished with a solid-surface countertop, offers plenty of space for socializing and games, as well as ample storage below for drinks and glassware. It's an item you can add to existing space as an independent improvement or incorporate into the design of a family room makeover.

◀ A stone fireplace and chocolate-tone walls lend texture and color to this entire room and set the stage for the dark tones of the built-in cabinets. The purpose of these dark colors is to set off the light blues of the stone fireplace and chimney. The cabinets on either side of the fireplace feature different door configurations, which add to the utility of the space and increases its visual interest.

6

FAMILY ROOMS

▶ One of the primary advantages of built-in cabinets is that they allow you to use space that might otherwise go unoccupied. This home office has been tucked into an angled recess at one end of the family room—with plenty of drawers, cabinets, and cubbyholes for financial records, working papers, and school supplies. The hardware on the upper cabinets differs from the base-cabinet knobs. Using different styles of drawer pulls adds interest to the doors and is one of the latest trends in cabinetry.

▶ This wall-to-wall built-in cabinet solves a number of storage puzzles. It provides ample space for the large flat-screen television and houses all the audiovisual gear that supports the entertainment center. Although the TV remains the center of attention in this unit, its space is balanced by the open shelves on both sides and the display space in the upper portions of the case.

◀ With a little creative imagination and a sense for maintaining the style of a room throughout, built-in storage can bring an added attractiveness to a room. This arts-and-crafts base unit does not actually support the ceiling, but adds to the sense of enclosure and separation between the two rooms—without making the unit seem bulky. The face of the unit is nicely broken up with different kinds of closed storage. The contrast between the solid doors, glass panels, and stacked drawers creates a pleasing visual rhythm on the face of the cabinet.

FAMILY ROOMS

▲ A built-in window bench adds a nice place to sit down in the corner of this family room and doubles as storage. In this model, access to the storage is accomplished by doors. In another situation, a hinged lid would work just as effectively. For information on how to construct a window seat with storage, see pages 176–181.

Freestanding units

O ne of the primary assets of freestanding storage units (apart from their lower cost) is flexibility. They can go anywhere—almost at a moment's notice. You can move them from place to place within a room to freshen up the arrangement or from room to room as your storage needs and style tastes change.

Freestanding units come in more types of structures too. While shelving (open and closed) is the predominant vehicle for built-ins, freestanding units can be armoires, hutches, bookcases, tables, trunks, and modular systems. This kind of variety makes your design and storage options almost endless. Some freestanding units even look like built-ins. You'll find this range of options handy when you plan your storage space.

As with any room, it pays to assess your family room storage needs before you start purchasing items. Sketch the room and draw in the storage solutions you want. Include the dimensions of the spaces, and carry the sketch with you when you shop.

▲ Bookcases come in a variety of styles and dimensions, so you shouldn't have to worry too much about finding one that fits your room to a T.

▶ When you consider the variety of freestanding shelves on the market, you'll realize that there are very few spaces they won't conform to. Here a combination of heights make a nice window surround for open storage display space.

▶ Hutches, pie safes, armoires, and antique highboys provide storage for anything you need to keep out of sight (or with glass fronts, on partial display). If you're converting an antique piece for modern use you'll probably have to beef up the thickness of the shelving or change the hardware to suit your style. (The shelves weren't made to carry the weight of things you'll put there.) Save the original pieces and don't make extensive modifications to an expensive piece—you'll reduce its value. For example, refinishing may make your pie safe look like new, but will destroy the quality that makes your treasured hutch valuable—its patina. In lieu of antique pieces, you'll find a host of modern updates like the one shown here.

▲ Don't overlook the storage potential of tables, tea carts, and trunks. Horizontal surfaces are ideal for temporary storage of family room items, such as games, books, newspapers, and decorative items. Trunks or even old suitcases in a stack can double as end tables while providing storage space inside.

GOOD IDEA

BOOKCASE TIPS
Bookcases won't be the answer to your storage problems if you let them get cluttered. Subdivide the space for smaller items, such as CDs or video tapes. Baskets and bins bring a nice decorative contrast to a bookcase, but whatever kind of container you use, keep the style consistent. For papers

and photos use neutral colors to create a unified, calm appearance, or brighten up the shelves with colored binders. Create the illusion of a built-in unit by butting two bookcases in a corner. Consider placing a doorway between two side units—just for display. Weed out your books and tapes periodically to free up additional storage space.

Entertainment centers

n almost all family rooms, the entertainment center functions as the focal point of the layout, and the television functions as the focal point of the entertainment center. Your version of an entertainment center can be as uncomplicated as a wall-mounted television with a shelf for a DVD player and audio equipment or as elaborate as a wall-to-wall enclosure that houses the television and all the supporting gear for a full-scale home theater with surround sound.

All of this brings up the question of where to store everything. The first thing you should do is decide what kind of equipment you want, then consider how to house it—not vice versa. Remember, too, that an entertainment center cabinet is not just a piece of furniture, it's likely to

dominate the entire design theme of your room. Make sure the style you pick is harmonious with the rest of the family room furnishings, or pick the cabinet and design the room around it.

You can make your own unit, have it made to your specifications, or purchase one of many ready-to-assemble units available at home centers and home furnishing stores. Measure the dimensions of the equipment you'll need and be sure it will fit the cabinet. Adjustable shelves are a must.

One other important decision to make before shopping—do you want the TV always visible or hidden behind doors when not in use? You might be able to retrofit doors onto a custom or home-crafted unit, but not onto a commercial one.

▶ This armoire demonstrates that your entertainment center does not need to occupy most of the room. Small units like these, with swinging or tambour doors, will house all the necessary gear, and do it in style. If you're short on space, don't overextend your entertainment storage needs. Stick with what fits. You can upgrade later if you want to.

◀ Although this commercial entertainment center appears to require extensive assembly, you can get your system housed and up and running in this unit in a weekend. Like most entertainment centers, this one is designed to hold all your equipment—CD player, DVD player, VHS recorder, audio amplifier, tuner, and power supply. The side panels even have room for a pair of speakers. Although this unit leaves the television exposed, you have a number of door options—tambour or swinging doors, and bifolds—if you want a way to keep it out of sight.

▶ Most television models in use today are so large that it's hard to keep them from dominating your design scheme. If you feel the appearance of this giant electronic "eye" intrudes on your space, either get a unit with doors or look at the TV space in the context of your overall design. The inclusion of drawers and especially open shelves—with their array of well chosen display items—broadens the focal point in the room. Anything you can do to make the area surrounding the television attractive will minimize its intrusion.

BUYER'S GUIDE

STORING ELECTRONIC GEAR

The first thing you need to remember about storing your audiovisual gear is that they generate heat—lots of it—and if you don't give each item enough room for air to circulate, you'll be making a return trip to your electronics supply store. For some electronic units, an inch all the way around is enough. For others, especially those with side vents, an inch might not do it. If the entertainment center doesn't come with vent holes in the back, cut them with a hole saw. Cut vent holes in the shelves, too, and be sure there's plenty of room for all the cables and wiring associated with home entertainment. If you purchase your gear at a big-box discount house, you're probably on your own as far as getting technical help. But the packaging on such purchases will usually contain information about the ventilation required.

▼ One thing you don't want in your family room is CDs and their cases spread out all over. One good way to store them is in a drawer, or independent unit with slots, that holds the cases so you can read the titles. Most ready-to-assemble entertainment centers will feature some form of CD storage. Cubic cases, other storage vehicles, and models similar to the one shown here can be purchased as freestanding units in a wide variety of styles.

On display

Bare walls do not a family room make. If you leave this room entirely functional—outfitted only with exercise equipment, furniture, and the entertainment center—you may find you don't use it as much as you imagined.

Creating an atmosphere conducive to relaxing is as important as putting furniture in the "right" place. Today's family rooms are often large, presenting you with lots of empty wall space (floor space, too, but here it's the walls that should get your attention). This is the perfect place to bring in open shelves, bookcases, free-hanging shelves, units with glass doors, and other items made for display. What goes on them? Photographs (in frames, of course), collections, artwork, vases, glassware, knickknacks, books, and boxes—but not in cluttered piles. This is a little like solving a storage puzzle in reverse—you have the space, now what goes in it? Well, anything you like the looks of and that contributes to an overall relaxed atmosphere. One thing that's important in laying out a display is to give each item enough room so it doesn't compete with others. Contrasts are good—of texture and color—and so is grouping like items in a particular area. A collection of antique toy banks, for example, shows off best when arranged in the same general space.

■ A glass-front unit creates the impression that what's behind it is somehow special and not for handling. Maybe it's similar to peeking through a keyhole because the sides of the doors frame the objects. You may want to keep items of value behind glass (and outfit the doors with locks if children are around). Glass doors provide a visual balance to almost every kind of furnishing, from the hutch and desk combination (above) to the drawer unit (left).

▲ The modular pieces of this modern display unit can be rearranged into different combinations or split into multiple units. The simple, clean look of this unit puts the emphasis on the items being displayed.

▶ This ladder display shelf adds a bit of architectural whimsy to your living space. Free-standing shelves can be rearranged like the furniture to give you limitless design potential, even in a small space. For safety's sake, once the unit is in place, attach it to the wall.

▲ When choosing shelving as a storage solution, remember that the piece that supports the shelf has as much to do with the style of the item as any other element. Brackets, also called corbels, serve both functional and decorative purposes. A complex and ornate carved bracket (above left) complements old-world styles such as Tuscan or Mediterranean. The hickory bracket (above center) contrasts nicely with the straight, narrow lines of the hickory beadboard. A fussy bracket would not look right in this location. Subtly scalloped brackets (above right) create a pleasing visual rhythm that helps call attention to the shelf and its contents.

◄ Nothing calls attention to a collection more effectively than shelves that don't call attention to themselves. Free-hanging shelves are the best for this kind of display. The shelf itself hides the support plate that holds it to the wall.

Offices and hobby rooms

Offices and hobby rooms have one advantage over other rooms—you can put them almost anywhere. However, no matter where you put them, they come with one imperative—they must be organized to provide maximum efficiency. If you have to spend time flipping through a stack of papers for an important document (while a client is waiting on the phone), or spend even five minutes looking for

the scissors or a tube of craft paint, it raises your stress level and reduces your productivity and enjoyment of the space.

If you don't have an office or hobby room yet but are planning one or both of these additions, the first thing you should do is make a list of all the activities that will take place in the space. Later you'll divide these activities into "zones" (yes, even offices have them). This will give you some idea of how much space you

Chapter 7 highlights

MATCHING OFFICE SPACE TO NEEDS
How much office space you need will depend largely on whether your home is your main place of business.

106

GETTING THE MOST FROM YOUR DESK
The desk is the most important surface in your office. Getting it to run "right" is the key to a successful workday.

110

STAYING ORGANIZED
Here it is again, that business of staying organized. Good storage can save you time and money. Where else is that more important than in a home office?

114

HOBBY ROOM STORAGE
Hobbies contain a lot of "things," and if you keep them organized your pursuits will be more enjoyable.

118

THE HOME WORKSHOP
Home workshops should be both productive and safe. Good storage helps keep them that way.

122

need. If there's an unused corner of the family room (and family activities won't interfere with your concentration), tuck your office or hobby room there. A family room location is a good place for mom or dad to work and still keep an eye on young children.

If you've run out of space, think about your basement, attic, or garage. These places often have large areas of unused space. Each of them may require some renovation, but that presents an opportunity in itself. You get to design the space just the way you want it. No more crawling around to plug things into long extension cords.

If you already have an office or hobby room that's a mess, start fixing it by gathering everything you can and get it to a place outside the work area. Set up a folding table nearby and haul the tumbled mass of things over to it. Then plan your space in activity zones (for example, composing, printing, scanning, faxing), move in any storage solutions you need (such as shelves or bookcases), and put the stuff where it belongs.

Matching office space to needs

How much space you'll need in your office depends to a large degree on how much time you will spend there. If all you need is an incidental place to make grocery lists, pay bills, and prepare taxes, you might find a corner in the kitchen. You'll need a small desk (perhaps large enough for a computer), a comfortable chair, and some drawers for a few files. Using a folding screen to conceal the space while you're working and after you're done will help give the room its own identity and keep work separated from other family activities.

If you work at home, either part or full time, you'll probably need an entire room—or the equivalent space. Two family members working means an even larger space, maybe enough for two computers. If you're just starting to design your office, be sure to include enough space on the desktop for all the computers, keyboards, phones, calculators, fax machines, printers, pencil sharpeners, lighting, and scanners. Then plan the desk space so you have ready access to each of them without having to slide one thing out of the way to get to the other. You'll also need storage for financial records, research material, bills, incoming and outgoing mail, and office supplies—paper, writing instruments, note pads, electronic storage (CDs/DVDs), and paper clips, just to mention a few.

GOOD IDEA

LAYING OUT THE LAYOUT
An L-shape office space will give you more accessible working room than a straight run. U-shape layouts are even more effective because they put more things within arm's reach—both arms.

■ Thinking "small" is perfectly OK when planning office space that will be used only for routine home "business"—paying bills, taxes, and preparing the list of weekly food purchases. Both of the office layouts shown here are adjacent to the kitchen and tucked conveniently in an alcove or corner. Each one takes a different, but equally effective, approach to storage—approaches that are largely a condition of the style of the room. Both cabinet styles are an extension of the kitchen cabinets. The raised melamine cabinets (left) came with cubbies just right for keeping pencils, notepads, and support materials within easy reach. The maple cabinets (below) keep all that stuff out of sight in closed units.

■ Both of these small-office solutions display features worth remembering when planning this kind of space. The office (above) also functions as a well-situated family communications center—it's part of the kitchen but well outside the work triangle. The maple office (right) provides an answer for offices that don't have enough space for a full-size desktop computer. Today's laptop computers are technological marvels, packing enormous capability into a small space. There's very little you can do on a desktop computer that you can't also do on a laptop.

7

OFFICES AND HOBBY ROOMS

◀ With a little ingenuity, you can transform cabinetry designed for the kitchen into a very comfortable, efficient home office. Spice drawers on the right of the layout are just right for storing pencils and small office supplies. Open shelving allows easy access to research materials, photos, and mementos, and the drawers keep paperwork and records out of sight. Outfit drawers with racks for sliding files so your paperwork stays organized and easy to use.

▲ Neat and tidy—that's the effect of a closed storage office system. Yet everything in this office layout is within easy reach. The printer and fax machine are removed from the central workspace, but close enough for comfort, and the bulletin board creates space for the calendar and notes that help keep work progressing smoothly.

▲ Here's a symmetrical solution to the problems associated with designing office space for two. The central table provides a common workspace, the two computers are networked to a shared printer, and even though the cabinetry is the same on both sides, it's clear that each person has created a workspace that reflects his or her identity.

▲ Everything in open storage is on display, and office organization has a tendency to quickly disintegrate—especially under the pressure of looming deadlines. If your office layout includes expanses of open shelving, you'll find it easier to keep it uncluttered if you use the shelves to store only those items you need frequently.

 WORK SMARTER

PAPER STORAGE
How long should you keep paper records? Here are some general guidelines.

- Tax returns—keep them forever. Store supporting documents for 4 years.
- Records of investment purchases—keep them for 3 years after you sell them.
- Cancelled checks—although they're becoming a thing of the past, keep tax-related checks with the rest of that year's documents. Anything else goes in the shredder after you've balanced your checkbook.
- Utility bills—shred upon payment unless the expense is business related. Then it's a tax document.
- Pay stubs—usually you only need the latest one to keep track of automatic "payment to date" deductions.
- Insurance policies—keep them for the life of the policy.

Getting the most from your desk

All office desks have one primary function—to provide a surface where work can be done effectively. Some desks have spaces for active and inactive storage, but organizing files comes later. Your first task is to organize your desktop for maximum efficiency.

Your computer is the first thing to locate. Generally it is in the center of the workspace, with the keyboard directly in line with it or slightly to one side or the other, on the desk or a sliding keyboard tray. Then the phone—generally it's best to put this on the side of the computer opposite your dominant hand (on the left for right handers). This allows you to grab and hold it while taking notes during the conversation, if necessary. Calculators go next—on the side where you'll use them. Almost all the rest of the desktop stuff is better kept in the organizer of your choice—cups or vertical containers for pens and

pencils, shallow containers for paper clips, vertical cubbies or dividers for notecards and letter-size envelopes—all within easy reach.

Peripherals come next. Place the printer so you can retrieve the printed material without getting up, or at least within a short scoot of your chair. The same goes for the scanner. Copier and fax machines (often one and the same) probably won't get as much use, so a convenient location is not as important for them.

Then comes the paper. Printer paper is best located close to the printer—flat pullout trays are a good place, but keep various sizes separated. Paperwork that needs to be stored should go either in active storage (file drawers nearby) or inactive (file boxes in a closet or remote location).

▶ Good looks and hardworking work space should be the benchmarks of a home office. A pullout keyboard tray keeps the desktop clear for paperwork. Wire-mesh containers in various configurations keep envelopes, pencils, and "work in progress" neat and accessible. Always resist the temptation to use your desktop as a temporary storage area—the belief that "you'll get to it later" only creates piles of clutter.

◀ Whether you need separate storage for your computer hard drive, or tower, depends on the computer model and your work style. If you want the tower out of sight, it can go in base cabinet space behind a door, or installed on a pullout tray. In any case, if you keep the tower in closed storage, open the door or pull out the tray when you use the computer so the hard drive gets enough air circulation. Today's computer chips generate much more heat than earlier versions.

WORK SMARTER

FILE ACCORDING TO YOUR STYLE

If you're the type who likes your paperwork out of sight, then get it behind closed doors (or drawers). If you like to see your files to remind you of what you need to do, then keep them arranged in vertical file dividers. Use a stair-stepped model to organize them by priority, or hang pocket organizers on the wall. Whatever device you use, keep as much as possible within easy reach.

■ If your business generates a steady flow of paperwork, keep the active files close at hand in file drawers. Hanging files—either for single drawers (above) or double-wides (right)—offer the most flexibility. Hanging folders come with their own tabs so you can keep your subfolders in categories of your choice. They also allow you to remove an individual file folder and put it back in the same place without having to search for the right spot again.

 GOOD IDEA

SIZING UP YOUR DESK
If you're in the market for a new desk or computer table, make sure it's large enough to house your computer, keyboard, and monitor. The desk should be deep enough to place the monitor at least 18 inches from your eyes. A standard-size monitor needs a depth of about 24 inches.

▶ This set of shallow pullout trays gets the "little stuff" off the desktop but keeps it handy. You could duplicate the efficiency of this unit in an existing base cabinet by adding a series of shelves and using shallow bins as your pullouts.

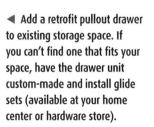

◀ Add a retrofit pullout drawer to existing storage space. If you can't find one that fits your space, have the drawer unit custom-made and install glide sets (available at your home center or hardware store).

 GOOD IDEA

WORKING UP TO GOOD STORAGE
Can't find enough room to house the printer, scanner, copier, and fax machine? Then stack them. Build a vertical shelving unit with space tailored to the size of each machine. Plan ahead so the spaces are large enough to accommodate new models when you get them.

Staying organized

O nce you have your office space organized, you're going to want to keep it that way. There are two general approaches to this problem—the idealistic path and the realistic one. The idealistic avenue prescribes putting everything back in its proper place immediately when done with it. If you're on the realistic avenue, you know you won't.

The first thing to try is to keep your desktop clear by not laying items down in any old place, thinking you'll file it later. Try to get in the habit of putting things away, including paperclips—right away. If you do leave your stuff around, do get to it later—at least once a day. Use the last 5 or 10 minutes of each day to put things back. That way you'll begin tomorrow with a fresh place to work. Get in the habit of going through your files each year and purging things you no longer need. Mark the date for this activity on your calendar and treat it as a business appointment you have to keep. A good time to do this is after you've filed your taxes.

Keep a recycling bin or basket—and a paper shredder—close to your work space. When the bin is full, shred the stuff and put it on the curb.

Make storage a habit with "habit helpers"—find (or make) the right containers for small things, such as paper, pencils, stamps, paper clips, and staples. A thing put in its proper place is a thing waiting to be used, not found.

◄ Cubbies, large and small, squat or tall, can solve a host of storage problems and keep you in the habit of putting your things in their designated spaces. After all, a habit is easier to develop and maintain the fewer excuses you have—in this case the fewer places you have for putting things. In fact, the home office illustrated (left) is founded almost entirely on the cubby principle. Everything that needs to be seen and used regularly is in plain sight. With this unit you can close up shop at the end of the day by closing the pocket doors. The rolltop desk (below), a take-off on the office standard of yesteryear, hides two rows of open spaces for the little things that tend to keep an office space disorganized.

 GOOD IDEA

CABINET COVER-UPS

Commercial file cabinets are an inexpensive vehicle for storing paperwork. Yet a lot of them are as unattractive as they are effective. Hide them behind homemade skirts. Fasten the skirt around the sides and back with hook-and-loop tape and make the front section a flap you can pull away or lay on top to open the drawers.

■ Keeping pencils and other instruments organized is a whole lot easier if you can separate the items from one another. Use tiered drawers with sliding trays—or just plain bin or plastic dividers—to group things of similar use. These shallow containers also help corral the various nonbusiness items from other parts of the house that seem to show up in the office.

▶ Doors hinged on their top edge are easy to use and help put under-cabinet space to effective use.

◄ The complete office should include some kind of mechanical "memory" to help you sort out tasks and keep track of things you need to do in the future. Here it's a cork board, but even a metal plate fastened to the wall and magnets will provide a home for notes and reminders.

▶ The pullouts and door racks normally found in kitchen pantry cabinets make great game room and hobby room storage units. The sturdy shelves and glides meant for pots and pans can easily hold heavy table games and toys.

Hobby room storage

Holy hobby room! If that's your reaction when you enter your hobby space and you can't find a horizontal surface, it's time to roll up your sleeves and get organized. This could be a more difficult task in a hobby room than in others. Hobbies have a lot of parts—bolts of fabric, fabric paint, paints and oils, brushes, cutting instruments, paper, canvases, spools of thread, pottery supplies, vases and buckets for floral arrangements, and chemicals and paper for the photographer.

The best thing you can do is get all the stuff out of the room before you try to organize it and put it back. If this proves impossible, at least tackle one section at a time. Bring in a folding table as a staging section and put the clutter there before you put it back.

Certain hobbies complete a piece in stages—for example, cutting, pinning patterns, stitching, sewing, and ironing for sewing. Sketch out your room and try to develop zones for each stage. Consider the things you need for each activity, decide the most appropriate storage vehicle, build or buy it, and move back in. As a general rule, small stuff goes in small containers and large stuff goes in large spaces, such as shelves. What's most important is that you get what you need close to the place you need it.

YOUR WORK SURFACE
Most hobbies and crafts require one or more work surfaces—a table, a bench, a slab door laid on file cabinets—something. Make sure your worktable is up to your standards—are you going to use it sitting down or standing up? How much weight will it have to support? Will it need a leg under the center to support additional weight? Will it need to be impervious to water and other liquids, and will it clean easily? For some hobbies in cramped quarters, you may be able to get by with a folding table stored behind the door—for a while. If that's a solution you're still using, consider another storage location. Maybe there's space in the attic, basement, or garage you haven't thought of. Or you might be able to maneuver into an unused walk-in closet.

7

OFFICES AND HOBBY ROOMS

■ The same general principles for storage in other rooms apply to hobby room storage. Use open shelves for things you need to see and use frequently, closed storage for items used less often. Tall bookcases can bail you out in a small room—they make good use of the vertical wall space, freeing up floor space for production. Items on open shelves should be categorized, and although they're not primarily "on display" in this room, orderly stacks or groups will help you see what you need. Besides, there's nothing wrong with adding splashes of color to the scene. Drawer units are great for flat storage like art papers and portfolios, or as large units for bins and small containers.

▶ Pegboards are not a panacea for all storage ills, but they sure come in handy for certain things, such as scissors, tools, special storage racks, and baskets. If you haven't looked at a pegboard recently, you'll find that the accessories for it have come a long way from that single odd-shape hook you had trouble slipping and snapping into the hole. You can now purchase shelf supports, racks, single and double brackets, and almost anything you need for your particular open storage needs.

▼ Open shelves are a good solution for those things you need on a regular basis. They give you the option of subdividing the space with tubs or other containers or leaving the items uncovered. Certain things should go in containers with lids; for example, fabrics and sewing supplies. Other materials, such as photo-developing chemicals (below right), need to be out in the open, but in a locked room.

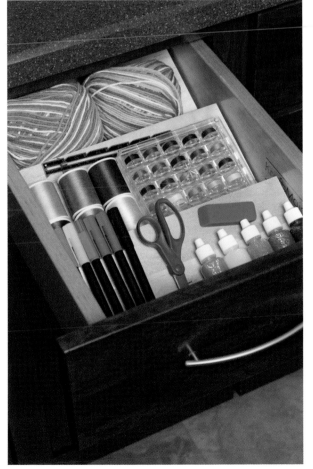

■ If you can divide your small things into sections, you will find them more easily. What's more, you avoid the trip to the hobby supply store to buy something you already have but can't find (then you'll have two of them to misplace). Drawer dividers come sized for deep or shallow drawers. Spice drawers can double as storage drawers for paints and glitter bottles. Baskets are small-scale pullouts just waiting to be put to use. If you're looking for ideas, start with kitchen accessory catalogues. You can employ many kitchen storage solutions in your hobby space with minimum expense and a cordless drill.

The home workshop

A room becomes a shop the minute you put a tablesaw in it. Even though you may not need many more tools than that (for a while), you'll need good storage immediately.

Storage is crucial to a smooth-running shop. There's no point in stumbling all over your tools while you try to work. Inexpensive metal or plastic shelves can hold your power tools when you're not using them. Fasten the shelves to the wall to keep them from tipping. Make a clamp rack by screwing a 2×4 to some blocks that you've screwed to the wall. Put your hand tools—the chisels, planes, screwdrivers, and wrenches that you collect along the way—in a good set of drawers. A mechanic's chest is ideal, but old kitchen cabinets, file cabinets, or even an old dresser will work too. The object here isn't to have the prettiest shop, or even the best shop. The object is to have a shop that works—so you can—without interruption.

In some ways, storage solutions will take care of themselves—or become a whole lot easier—if you organize your shop into work zones. You'll want storage for raw materials, hardwoods and sheet goods, and for each of the other workstations—layout, cutting, assembling, and finishing. If you're short on space, put your stationary power tools on wheels and move them to the stations when you need them. You can also put your storage containers on wheels and move them to the tools.

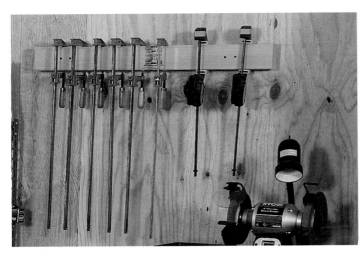

▲ You'll need a variety of storage solutions for your home workshop and you can make some of them yourself. Keeping clamps in order is easy with a 2×4 fastened to the wall. Put a couple of 1× or 2× spacers behind it to give the clamps enough surface to hang on.

■ All manner of storage containers are available at your home center or hardware store—from specialty racks for screwdrivers and chisels to a variety of plastic and metal units with small compartments (above and left).

Sharing the shop

If there is no space in the basement for your workplace, and you have to share the garage with cars, bikes and the lawnmower, you still can set up shop. Many of the items taking up space in your garage can be placed into wall and base cabinets. You will be more tempted to return your workshop tools to their proper places on a visible pegboard. Add a work surface over the base cabinets and you have a modest but functional workshop.

Utility spaces

Uncluttering utility spaces, such as the garage and laundry room, is, as for all rooms, a process. Getting started may actually be the toughest part of the job. The best thing you can do to get you over the "I really don't want to do it" hump is to sketch your utility area roughly to scale and create zones on your diagram—tools and workbench in one area, garden implements and the potting bench in another. Zones for a laundry room might include—incoming, sorting, washing, drying (with racks and other appliances), folding, ironing, supplies, and a utility sink.

Take your sketch to your home center or retailer and shop for the items that will solve your storage problems—strong, sturdy shelving that can be mounted to the wall, vertical drawer units (on wheels if they're large and you need the mobility, stackable if they're small), wall and base cabinets, pegboards, hooks of all kinds, and waterproof tote bags for sports stuff.

To begin, pull out everything (pick a sunny day for the garage project). This gives you a clean slate, so to speak.

Wipe down all the shelves, sweep the floor, and hose down the garage. (Like a car, garages and laundry rooms seem to "run" better when they're clean.) Assemble and install your storage solutions in the areas noted on your sketch. Then start sorting.

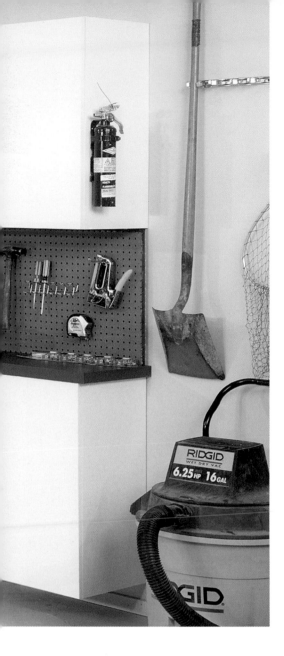

Chapter 8 highlights

LAUNDRY ROOMS
Clean, well lit, and efficient—these qualities are easy to achieve for a home laundry.

126

MAKING YOUR (LAUNDRY) LIFE EASIER
Small improvements in your laundry can make your tasks much easier.

130

GARAGE STORAGE
Garages can become the behemoths of storage problems. But you can tame them as easily as any other room. The same principles and methods apply here.

134

YARD AND GARDEN TOOLS
Good gardening requires good storage. The plants won't know it, but the gardener will.

138

SPORTS EQUIPMENT AND HOUSEHOLD GOODS
Sports equipment never seems to have a place of its own. Bags of it seem to grow just about anywhere. Find your preferred spot to keep the items contained.

140

OUTDOOR SHEDS AND BINS
Outdoor storage can be stylish and protective at the same time. There are a number of units you can assemble to keep your outdoor stuff in tow.

144

Put "don't-need-this" items to the side for trash pickup (probably more of these in the garage than the laundry)—and leave them there. This is no time to be sentimental. And make sure you put the items you retain in the places where you'll find them most useful. That's the reason for organizing the space into zones in the first place. It automatically creates an area in which pertinent things belong. Right from the start, zoned storage implements the keep-it-close-to-where-you'll-use-it principle (see page 12).

Laundry rooms

Laundry rooms are a storage puzzle all their own. They're often the smallest room in the house, they contain fewer things than kitchens and baths, and you'd think they'd be the easiest to organize. They actually are, but they rank down by the garage on the list of things to do. That's probably because the stuff in a laundry room is always in one state of transition or another, and there is always something more important to do with it than store it.

One of the easiest ways to make this space more effective is to hang wall cabinets (leftovers from the kitchen renovation?) above the washer and dryer. Solid or wire shelves will do too. Here's where the detergent, bleach, fabric softener, and other supplies go—right where you need them.

Whether you're using cabinets, shelves, or a wire system, incorporate some kind of bar into your design—for hanging clothes when they come from

the dryer. You can slip a tension rod between the cabinets (but be careful its lateral pressure doesn't break the side of the cabinets) or hang it in recessed blocks or flanges. Screw hooks on the bottom of shelves. Most wire systems include a way to hang a rod on the shelf.

Laundry baskets? They should go in the rooms where the dirty clothes collect. Equip each bedroom closet with baskets or sorter bags with metal frames—one bag for colored clothes, another for whites, and a third for delicates where appropriate. Have each person drop their clothes into the right basket and they will arrive in your laundry room presorted. (Make sure the kids take the crayons out of their pockets.)

Keep the room clean—no soap-spill residue, no dust, no loose feathers from bedding. A damp sponge will take care of most of these problems with one swipe.

■ Wire shelving keeps laundry supplies within easy reach. Some shelf models (left) come with a hanging rack built-in, so you can set shirts and other items best not folded out to dry. The open space between the dryer and wall keeps laundry baskets and towel storage out of the working floor space. A closet (above) is nice if your laundry room is on the second floor or in a high traffic area off the garage.

▲ The raised front-loading washer and dryer reduce extra bending and stooping. Controls at the front make appliances accessible for a person using a wheelchair and more comfortable for all users.

WORK SMARTER

RUNNING A SMART LAUNDRY

Washing clothes may not be the high point of your day. However, a raised washer and dryer and convenient laundry center make these chores easier.

Raising the height of the washer and dryer also helps you avoid excess bending. You can effortlessly toss clothes into a front-loading washer (which uses less detergent), and a front-loading dryer. The tops of both come in handy as counter space. Make sure the lint catcher is in front for easier cleaning.

Extend convenience into your closets. Install adjustable-height shelving (great for growing kids) and hang clothing on a motorized clothing carousel. Double racks in closets allow for less reach and more storage space.

▶ In a small home or apartment, the laundry room often is part of the bathroom, with a linen closet thrown in too. Wire shelving can be designed to make this small space attractive as well as functional. The rolling rack can slide in to hold bath linens or out to pick up dirty laundry around the house.

▼ Closed storage units work equally well in any laundry with enough space for them. Wire systems may be more flexible in small spaces, but if you have the room and want to keep everything out of sight, then cabinets are the way to go. Their function is the same as open storage—laundry supplies are housed in the wall cabinet above the washer and dryer. Base cabinets provide space for cleaning supplies and some remote storage for the towel overflow from the bathroom.

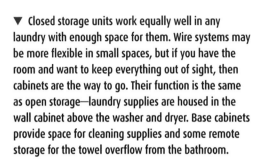

▲ To get this dryer positioned for a comfortable swing of the door, it had to be located away from the wall. This opened up space on the floor that could be used for laundry baskets or a narrow table or shelves.

► Ready-to-assemble laundry racks come in a variety of styles and sizes to fit the needs and space of almost any laundry room. They can function, as this one does, as an all-in-one clothing and supply rack. They're especially useful for clothes that need to be mended, keeping them separate from the rest of the laundry while providing you with a visual reminder that they need your attention. Add wheels and a rack like this allows you to move your work to a different room— to the family room, for example, if you want to do your repair work while watching your favorite movie.

◄ This expanse of ready-to-assemble wall cabinets seems like more than enough storage space for a small laundry. Cabinets over the washer house the laundry supplies, but the additional cabinets provide a remote storage home for items in the household that won't fit in other rooms.

Making your (laundry) life easier

I n just a standard 12½×6 foot laundry space, you can create an attractive utility hub that makes clothing care a breeze and doubles as a crafts or gift-wrap center!

Start with surfaces
Walls painted in semigloss white and floors covered with ceramic tile in light tones make easy cleanup of splashes, spills, and dirt from incoming laundry. Add a white utility tub as a water source for stain soaking, then bring in surfaces on which to fold clothing, stack laundry baskets, and store supplies.

Function looks good
Crisp, white surfaces plus baskets in bold, vibrant colors—red, blue, green, and yellow—give this space a fresh and energizing ambience. Enliven the space even more with red café curtains at the window and a bold-hued poster. Paint the pegboard red to match too.

Store it here
Room to spare? Your laundry room can also be home to household cleaning supplies, plant care and potting supplies, and shoe, leather, and suede care items. Second floor laundries are also a good place to stash an extra pencil, screwdriver, and hammer.

▲ Clean clothing goes straight into a basket—one for each family member—ready for pickup. Everyone can do his or her own folding on the melamine shelf above. Items that no longer fit go into the "donate" basket.

▲ Most of us would be more likely to fix a hem or sew a button on a shirt—now—if the needle, thread, and scissors leapt into our hands. That's pretty much what they do when stored on a section of white pegboard mounted to the wall. A laundry guide posted on the cabinet door takes the guesswork out of stain removal. On the shelves, plastic baskets corral supplies for specific laundry tasks, such as lint removal and ironing, and can be pulled out as needed.

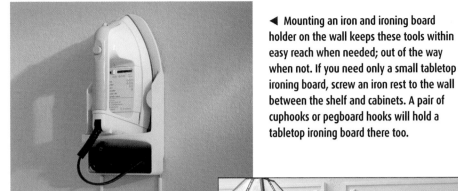

◀ Mounting an iron and ironing board holder on the wall keeps these tools within easy reach when needed; out of the way when not. If you need only a small tabletop ironing board, screw an iron rest to the wall between the shelf and cabinets. A pair of cuphooks or pegboard hooks will hold a tabletop ironing board there too.

▶ Speaking of out of the way, bifold doors (styled to look like paneled doors) hide the laundry center from the kitchen, avoiding an unnecessary visual distraction. They also don't take up as much floor space as the wide swing of hinged doors.

 GOOD IDEA

THE LAUNDRY THAT DOES MORE THAN CLOTHES
This room may be small, but you can turn it into a gift-wrap and crafts center with just a few extra fittings. Here's how:

- Mount white pegboard over the entire space between cabinets and shelving and hang scissors, tape, ribbon, tags, and craft supplies.

- Mount another rectangle of pegboard over the opposite wall space (away from water) and drop dowels horizontally into peg hooks to support rolls of gift wrap.

- If you must mount pegboard for paper goods near water, protect supplies from potential spray by dropping a protective panel from hooks at the board's two top corners. Use a cut-to-size piece of tarp, vinyl, or plastic fitted with grommets, or hanging loops, as the panel.

- Add a second work surface by protecting the washer and dryer top with a soft-backed vinyl tablecloth cut to size. This material is also sold by the yard at fabric stores. For a no-slip cover, cut the vinyl a few inches longer on each end, then use pieces of adhesive-back hook-and-loop tape to secure it to the appliance sides.

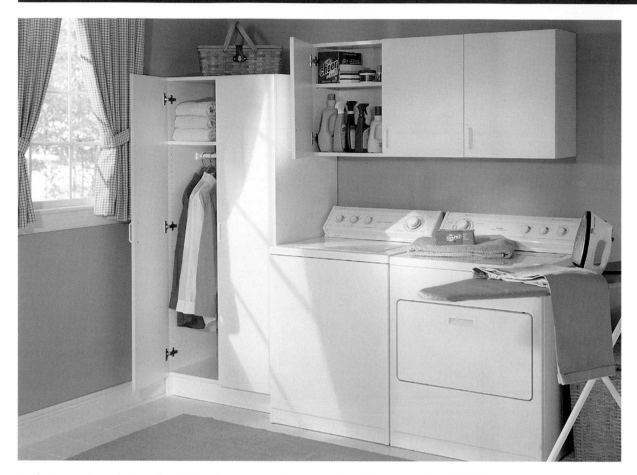

▲ The inexpensive melamine cabinets in this laundry room solve a small-space problem by making good use of the area above the washer and dryer. If budgets or timelines are tight, wire shelving can be a good replacement for wall cabinets. With a surface for folding clothes (as soon as possible after they come out of the dryer), you'll cut your ironing time in half. Experiment with the height of the clothes-folding table. Standard is 36 inches, but you may want it higher or lower.

► A plastic utility tub fitted with a basic faucet and sprayer is a low-cost way to bring sink and water service to a laundry room. When all the room's elements are white, it looks sharp as well. With a surface for folding clothes (as soon as possible after they come out of the dryer) you'll cut your ironing time in half. Experiment with the height of the clothes-folding table. Standard is 36 inches, but you may want it higher or lower than that.

◄ There's no sense in storing detergents in a closed cabinet if you need them at the washer. Setting detergents in a slim wheeled cart keeps them handy where they're needed. Pop-up hampers are terrific for incoming laundry from bedrooms. These hampers squish flat when not in use.

💡 GOOD IDEA

TRASH CONTAINMENT
Don't forget to include a trash can near the dryer so you can throw away used fabric softener sheets, lint, empty soap and bleach containers, stain sticks, and—every now and then—the contents of a kid's pockets.

► White's in style—the more attractive your space, the more you'll like working there and keeping it organized. Imagine, for example, how this laundry room would look, cluttered with clothes and supplies. The blue tile insets contrast subtly with the white wall tiles and carry out the classical design theme of the cabinetry. Fluorescent under-cabinet fixtures put light where you need it—an easy retrofit with fluorescent units you can buy at a home center.

Garage storage

Because your garage probably functions as the repository of things from other areas in the house you don't quite know what to do with, it's unlikely that you've formed strong attachments to much of its contents. An absence of sentiment will make decluttering it easier. (If you haven't already, go back and read pages 8–9 for suggestions on how to start weeding out any collection of surplus stuff.)

Even in an expansive space, garages can get so cluttered there's no room for the car. That's often because garages have to store so many different kinds of equipment—gardening and lawn care tools, recycling bins, automotive tools and supplies (like cleaners and waxes), home improvement tools and materials, sports gear, and general hardware. Use these categories to establish work and storage zones in your garage.

Sturdy is the watchword here. Garage storage takes a beating. Many stored items are heavy, many are made of metal, and the combination of weight and material can exact a toll on your storage solutions.

Buy heavy-duty cabinets with solid doors and plastic or steel shelving whose materials are thick and strong enough to support their own weight without careening from side to side. (No matter what the quality of free-standing shelves, fasten them to the wall to keep them from tipping over.)

Back to zones for a moment—if you can't create a large physical separation between them (with one zone on one wall and another across the garage) try to find a way to give each zone its own identity. The type of storage units and devices you choose will help this process.

◀ Sturdy wire racks and wood cabinets make a nice combination of open and closed storage. The racks can hold almost anything, but what you want here are the items you need to be able to see and access frequently. Large power tools, such as routers and belt sanders, can go in the cabinets below.

Garage organization tips

Garage space is full of opportunities for storage. Here are a few solutions you may find useful in organizing it.

■ Make maximum use of wall space. Floor space is for productive activities. The same kind of organizational systems designed for closets can easily solve garage storage puzzles. Use caution here. Some closet systems are strong enough only for storage of lightweight items, and many manufacturers offer a heavier line for garage storage. Bracket-and-track systems offer you the advantage of hefty support with the flexibility of adjustable shelves. Just make sure to fasten the track into the studs. Even more versatile are hanging systems made with horizontal brackets that will accept hangers specifically designed for tools, rakes, shovels, and bicycles—about anything you can think of.

■ Make your own garden tool hanging system by nailing a 2×4 to the studs and placing pairs of nails wide enough to accept the rake and shovel handles. As an alternative, use snap-in handle brackets.

■ Don't forget ceiling space. This is often the most untapped area in a garage. Make a floor of 1× stock across the ceiling joists and hoist lidded tubs, boxes, and other items up for permanent storage. There are also a host of ceiling storage systems that allow you to categorize your stuff in sections.

▲ Stack and store tools and supplies using a heavy-duty steel cabinet system like the one shown here. For drawer units, look for those that ride on ball-bearing glides.

■ A combination of modular closed storage units and shelves (above) transforms empty wall space into a balanced, all-purpose storage solution for garden supplies, recreation gear, and home improvement implements. An equally efficient option is shown (below)—a combination of cabinetry and heavy wire racks. Systems available at your home center and other retailers can be mixed and matched to conform to your needs or used in their entirety. There's not a garage built that wouldn't benefit from one of these solutions.

8

UTILITY SPACES

■ Pegboards have been around for a long time and their versatility keeps improving the longer they're in use. What they do best is to turn a wall into a vertical shelf. You can put up a small board for a small tool collection or convert an entire wall with them. Painted, they create a background that makes the tools more visible while adding a large splash of color. (Who says garages can't be stylish?) If you're hanging them on drywall, install 1× furring strips first so there's room behind the board for the foot of the hooks. If the studs are exposed, just screw the pegboard to the studs. As shown in these two examples, they work best when located in conjunction with a workbench or shelf to put tools on temporarily when you're not using them for a project.

Yard and garden tools

Store rakes, shovels, hoes, and spades on the floor in a corner, and when you grab one, you get them all. Store them vertically in a device made specifically for each one and retrieval is a breeze. And today you'll find devices galore. Manufacturers have come up with innumerable innovations for storing garden tools. Racks, racks with hooks, hooks on wire frames, strap hangers, and simple things like the wire-rack version of the nails-in-a-board used by your grandfather are all available. They are easy to install, easy to look at, and create effective storage.

You don't necessarily have to wait for a trip to the home center to find a storage solution. You can create homebrew storage solutions of your own. Shelving supported on the wall with 1×4s and 2×4s cut on the diagonal is a perfect DIY project—and you can pretty them up with a couple of coats of that left over white paint you've been wondering what to do with. Or take that 20-inch length of scrap 1×4 that's laying on your workbench, paint it to match the wall, and with a few strategically placed finishing nails, you've got yourself a rack for rakes and long-handled tools. This unit and its contents may be light enough that you don't have to fasten it to the studs, but you'll be better off doing so. And even if the handles have holes in the end, don't hang the utensils in the holes. Cut pieces of leather or cord and tie them in the holes. Loops hang things more quickly.

Remember the universal storage rule: Most people use 20% of their items 80% of the time. What's not used just takes up space.

◄ For things that won't hang, such as pots, pesticides, watering cans, and planters, use shelving. You can incorporate hangers into many shelf systems, and of course you can get these systems individually. This system relies on a series of bars fastened to the wall at prescribed intervals. Hundred of devices designed for specific tools attach themselves to the bars. Because the bars are sturdy, and spread the weight across the entire wall framing, you can hang some pretty heavy items on this wall yet move them easily.

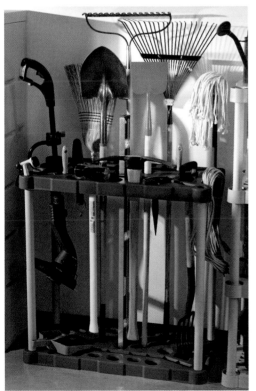

■ Vertical caddies (far left) are a gardener's delight. They can store a varying number of tools all pushed back neatly in the corner. Some are made of metal, others are plastic, but both materials are heavy-duty enough to last for a long time. If you're short on floor space but have room on the walls, store your long-handled tools on wall hanging racks (left).

Sports equipment and household goods

If tripping over a bike in the garage or stumbling over an errant ball doesn't show your cycling or soccer skills at their best, you may be tempted to put these items back in the house. Stop for a moment. This may not be a good solution. There's probably more storage space in the garage than in the house. The problem is, you don't have it organized yet.

Vertical modular cabinets come in a number of sizes, many of them tall and wide enough for a whole team's worth of hockey sticks or baseball bats, along with helmets, gloves, kneepads, balls, and other accoutrements of the sport. For a multisport family, get one for each sport. Your troubles and stumbles are over. Wall-mounted or freestanding racks are also a good solution.

■ This caddy (above) is right for housing the equipment for a number of sports. Sticks insert into the holes of the caddy, and the tennis balls, soccer balls, and hockey pucks go in the mesh duffel bag below. Whatever won't fit goes on the open shelf to the left.

Sometimes all of the floor space in the garage is needed. Track systems (left) are an excellent way to get even larger items, such as bikes, scooters, and golf bags, off the floor to make way for the car (or the new boat!).

■ Track systems offer unusual flexibility in solving storage problems. The tracks are designed to engage metal hooks and the hook assemblies take whatever form is necessary to hang hockey gear (above), shelves for household goods (upper left), and even bicycles (below left).

GOOD IDEA

STORING RECYCLABLES
Almost every kind of work done in a garage will create waste, and you'll need to accommodate it as trash or, depending on your community, as recyclable material. Be sure to include containers for this stuff—30 gallon trash cans with lids and plastic liners, pullout bag frames under a base cabinet, or a rolling wire rack or bin with several levels that will allow you to sort as you go.

■ Shelving comes in many forms and shapes, each designed to add a different kind of convenience to your storage needs. Plastic shelves (right) assemble in minutes (some with no tools) and feature differently shaped shelves to accommodate different household materials. Closed vertical units (below) are ideal for paints, chemicals, and other hazardous materials. Because of the configuration of the shelves inside, the same unit can serve different purposes.

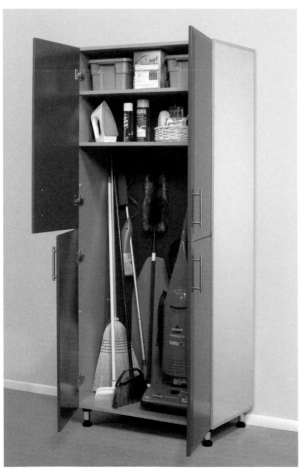

■ Ready-to-assemble closed storage cabinets come in a variety of styles. This basic cabinetry style is a truly no-hassle solution for storing equipment, household goods, and tools. Before you buy your shelving, make a plan for what you want to put in the cabinet. Gather those things together and measure the dimension of the items. If they won't stack, set them out on the floor as you would arrange them on the shelves. Measure the space they require (adding a couple inches all the way around), post the dimensions on a sketch, and take it with you shopping. Then buy the item that meets your specs, bring it home and assemble it. Put the stuff back, close the doors, and that's it. Problem solved in a couple hours.

Outdoor sheds and bins

In many ways, what won't fit inside must go outside. This is especially true if your garage is small or you don't have one at all. But it's also true if you're a gardener who wants to store tools closer to the garden. Or if you're an outdoor cook who needs to keep the grill, propane, and cooking utensils outdoors, but out of the rain. Or a home mechanic whose fix-it space is not in the garage but back behind it on a concrete pad.

Not too long ago, if you needed one of these storage units (mostly called sheds) outside, you'd have to build it yourself—that is, plan it, draw it, get a permit for it, get it inspected, and construct it from the ground up.

Then came a host of metal sheds, ready-made in the dimensions most commonly needed. Metal sheds are still around, in even more models than before, but you now have plastic buildings at your disposal. You may not get quite the satisfaction that you would from building your own, but the ease with which you can get these storage facilities up and running and the years they will serve with virtually no maintenance will make up for that loss of a creative expression.

◄ Once you get your outdoor stuff in your plastic shed, you're going to want to keep it organized and neat. Manufacturers have anticipated this and have come up with accessories that will accommodate a variety of storage needs. Larger lawn and garden tools will hang nicely on this rack and are easily accessible. Shelf brackets provide storage for other items, such as hand tools and potting soil.

▼ "Weighing in" at 7 feet square (49 square feet) and almost 8 feet high, this large resin shed will give your yard and garden clutter a place to go. You can store your lawnmower, garden supplies, and equipment with room to spare. This unit comes with its own floor and you can put it together in about an hour. You can lock it, too, but you'll have to buy the lock separately.

■ Sheds and bins come in all forms and sizes, some with hinged lids for access (right), others with doors (below right). The style and size you get should adequately hold your things—with additional room for the future ("Once you build it, they will come"). You don't want to carry a unit home, assemble it, and realize something you wanted in it won't fit. Before you make your purchase, it's wise to gather the things you plan to store, and lay them out on a flat surface. If the storage unit has one or more shelves, then your stuff should be divided into that number of sections. Measure the space the stored items take and then get a unit larger than their overall dimensions.

▲ Wood storage units have not disappeared into the dark recesses of storage history. They're still around, and you can buy units like this one ready to assemble. They make effective and attractive storage for deck and patio locations.

CHOOSING THE RIGHT SHED

Looking for some guidelines on choosing a shed? Here are a few tips.

■ Finding a shed to fit in with the architecture of your home should be fairly easy with one of the kits designed for this purpose. Before you choose the frills, however, you need to make a material decision. Metal buildings finished with a durable baked-on paint are less expensive than buildings made with vinyl-coated steel. Even heavier buildings are made for damage-prone areas. Metal will bend when bumped and may chip a painted unit. Repair this quickly to keep it from rusting. Vinyl is usually more expensive than steel but more durable too. Its surface won't peel or rust. Wood can be made fairly weatherproof with the proper finishes. Your construction and material costs will be more, but you don't have to worry too much about durability. After all, there are properly maintained wood structures still around after a couple hundred years.

■ Consider the size of the door opening. Double doors are worth any extra expense. They make loading and unloading far easier than pinching things through a single door.

■ Choose a location convenient to the place where you'll use the stored materials, keeping it out of high-traffic areas and places where kids play. The site should be smooth and level—a gravel or concrete base will increase the life of the structure. In many areas you will have to add a tie-down to keep the building from going off with a high wind.

8

UTILITY SPACES

Storage projects

How'd you like to solve your storage problems in a weekend, building all the units yourself, from start to finish? In many ways, that's what a large part of the storage industry has become—providing products and systems that average homeowners can install themselves. Start on Saturday and be done by Sunday night (or before).

If you've never worked on projects like this, when all the parts and all those little bags of hardware tumble out of the box, it can cause instant confusion. Some of these systems go together with fasteners that look similar to screws and bolts.

To avoid confusion, use some of the same organizational skills you've picked up sorting. Put similar pieces in stacks, dump out all the hardware and sort it into categories, and compare it to the parts list that came with the system (some are illustrated). Make sure everything is there. Sometimes it's not and you can get by without a piece until later, but if you need the missing object in step one, you'd better go back to the store and get it.

Then read through the section of this chapter that shows you how to put your system together, following the instructions step by step. You'll be done in no time.

Chapter 9 highlights

FASTENERS AND FASTENING

With accurate information about fasteners, you won't make the mistake of putting something up that will quickly come down.

150

LEVEL MOUNTING EVERY TIME

There's nothing more distracting than a shelf that's not level. It will draw your eye to it every time.

152

ASSEMBLY ESSENTIALS

There are certain assembly methods that are common to a number of storage solutions. They're quick and easy to learn.

154

INSTALLING WALL SHELVES

Here's where one method gets modified for shelves of different styles. Learn how to install freestanding, track-mounted, and bracketed shelving.

156

INSTALLING TRACK-MOUNTED WIRE SYSTEMS

Track-mounted wire shelving goes up in a flash with just a few hand tools.

158

INSTALLING CLIP-MOUNTED WIRE SYSTEMS

Clip-mounted shelving requires minimal layout and produces a handsome, sturdy storage solution.

160

INSTALLING MELAMINE CLOSET SYSTEMS

Melamine systems rely on some fastening innovations that are virtually foolproof.

162

ADDING PULLOUT SHELVES

Pullouts provide ingenious solutions to all kinds of storage problems.

164

FREESTANDING CABINETS AND SHELVES

Freestanding shelves are ideal for those storage solutions where low cost and ease of access are important.

170

ASSEMBLING PLASTIC STORAGE UNITS

Plastic storage units snap together, screw together, assemble on their backs and fronts—not trickier, just different from other units.

174

BUILDING A WINDOW STORAGE SEAT

A do-it-yourself project that adds seating, storage, and style to your home.

176

CONSTRUCTING CUBIC STORAGE UNITS

Modular units add a nice contemporary accent to any wall.

182

All of this assumes, of course, that you've already picked out your unit. If you haven't, this chapter can still come in handy. It lets you see up close what the final result will look like and it will give you some idea of what skills you need to get it together. You may find one system easier to install than another and base your decision solely on that. Use this chapter to preview the task and keep it with you as you work through it.

Fasteners and fastening

ehind every wall in your home is a series of studs—2×4s or 2×6s that hold up the walls. When you fasten shelves, closet systems, or cabinets to the studs, you can have confidence the unit will stay there.

Studs are generally placed 16 or 24 inches apart (measuring from center to center). With that in mind, once you've located one stud, finding the others is easy. Studs actually measure less than their stated dimensions. For example, a 2×4 actually measures $1\frac{1}{2}$ inches by $3\frac{1}{2}$ inches.

Choosing fasteners

The correct fastener depends on your home's finished wall material. They're likely made of drywall if your home was built after the 1950s. Homes built before then generally have plaster and lathe walls, though some have been remodeled with drywall. If you're not certain, remove a switch or outlet plate and look at the wall's cut edge. A flat white panel is drywall. Narrow strips of wood behind a whitish surface form a plaster and lathe wall.

Regardless of your wall material, if you can fasten to a stud, you should use a screw. Drywall screws are a terrific choice for studs behind either type of wall. Their sharp points and deeply threaded shaft make them similar to, but superior to, nails. All that banging with hammer and nails can be pretty tough on wall material.

UN-STUDDED SUPPORT

There's not always a stud where you need it. That's where toggle bolts and drywall anchors come in: Use an anchor in drywall, a toggle bolt in either drywall or plaster.

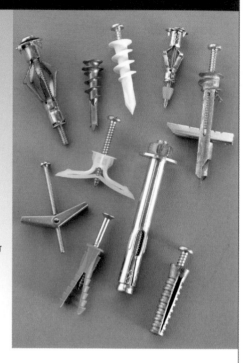

Finding the studs

1

"SEEING" THROUGH THE WALL

Look for fastener marks in the wall or tap on the wall with your knuckle. Where you see a fastener or where you hear the sound deaden somewhat, that's where to start. Roll the stud finder over the wall; the light blinks green when it senses something stopping the beam. That's the stud. Fine-tune your position to locate the center of the stud and mark it.

2

MAKE YOUR FIRST MARK

It's important to nail or drill directly into the center of a stud—if it's off to one side, a fastener can sliver a stud and it won't hold your artwork or shelving. Measure out $\frac{3}{4}$ inch from your center mark and draw vertical lines to represent the edges of the stud. You can add an "X" to make the center mark more visible.

3

MARK THE REMAINING STUDS

In most homes studs are spaced either on 16- or 24-inch centers. Measure 16 inches from the first stud, and check the location with the stud finder. if there's not one there, measure at 24 inches and repeat the process. If you still can't find one, repeat the process until you locate the next stud and mark it—even if it's spaced differently than others.

Installing a hollow wall anchor

1 DRILL THE HOLE

Enlarge the center mark you made by tapping a nail or nail set directly on the mark. This will help prevent the drill from wandering. Set the tip of the drill in the enlarged hole and drill slowly, until the bit pushes through the surface or deep enough to hold the anchor. Self-tapping and nail-point anchors don't need a drilled hole. Just screw them or hammer them into your center mark.

2 DRIVE THE SCREW

Push the anchor into the hole and tap it flush with a hammer. Insert the screw into the anchor and drive it as far as you need to hold the object. For some shelves or other items, you will have to insert a bracket or tab on the screw before driving it. Tighten the screw only till it's flush with the top of the anchor.

DRIVING THE FASTENER

When you're driving the fastener, go slowly. There is a lot going on behind the scene. As the screw is sunk, it opens the anchor flanges on the other side of the drywall, providing a tight bond with the material.

Installing a toggle bolt

1 DRILL THE HOLE

Just as you would for a hollow wall anchor, enlarge the center mark with a nail or nail set and drill the hole until the bit pushes through the surface.

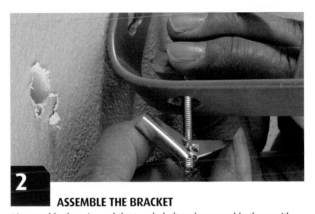

2 ASSEMBLE THE BRACKET

Disassemble the wings of the toggle bolt and reassemble them with the screw inserted in the bracket hole.

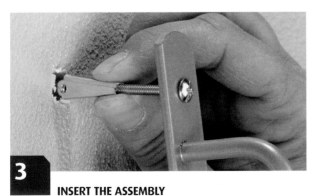

3 INSERT THE ASSEMBLY

Fold the wings up and insert the toggle into the wall. Push the screw until you hear the wings snap open. Pull on the screw to make sure. It should not come out.

4 TIGHTEN THE BOLT

Pull back on the bolt to keep the wings from spinning on the opposite face of the wall. Turn the bolt by hand till it becomes hard to turn. Then snug it with a screwdriver.

Level mounting every time

9

STORAGE PROJECTS

H ang a shelf, display ledge, or cabinet level and its neat appearance will have you feeling smug every time you see it; hang it crooked and you'll frown—or have to rehang it a little higher or lower. Getting it right the first time is easy if you mark and measure with care and drill your screw holes precisely.

1 MAKE YOUR MARK
Use a sharp pencil to mark the wall at the center location of your first fastener.

2 MEASURE THE CENTERS
Using a tape measure, measure the distance between the centers of the fasteners on the object you want to hang. Jot down the measurement. Then measure it again, to make sure.

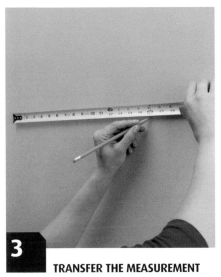

3 TRANSFER THE MEASUREMENT

Again using the tape measure (the same one—don't switch measuring instruments in midstream), mark the fastener spacing on the wall. Try to get the marks as level as you can by eyeballing the situation.

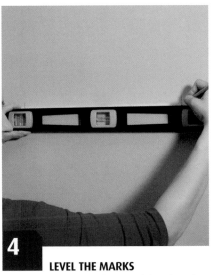

4 LEVEL THE MARKS

Hold your spirit level with one end directly under the mark for the first fastener. Move the other end of the level up or down until the center bubble is centered in its vial. Mark a horizontal line directly through the second fastener location.

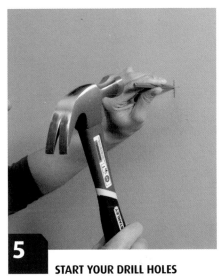

5 START YOUR DRILL HOLES ON TARGET

Use your hammer and a nail or center punch to expand your center marks slightly. Hold the nail or center punch perpendicular to the wall and tap it hard enough to make a dimple to press your drill bit into.

6 DRILL AWAY

Insert the drill bit in the chuck, tighten the chuck, put the drill into forward gear, place the drill point in the dimple, and check to make sure the drill bit is perpendicular to the wall. Drill the hole. Holding the drill in place, put it in reverse to back out cleanly without disturbing the wall material. Install the fasteners and hang the shelf.

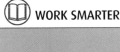 WORK SMARTER

USING A LASER LEVEL

Relatively new to the consumer scene, laser levels are quickly overtaking spirit levels as the leveling tool of choice. Lasers are easier to use and can project level lines down the length of a room and all the way around it. Prices for laser levels begin at less than $30, and you can find them with stud-finding features. Most models either press against the wall or are fastened to a tripod.

Assembly essentials

Assembling something today? Resist the urge to dump everything out of the box and begin putting things together, no matter how easy it may seem. Take just a few minutes; follow these tips to spare yourself hassle and confusion later.

- Lay out all components. Read the instruction sheet; make sure all pieces and fasteners are present.
- Check all pieces to make sure nothing was damaged in shipping.
- Set all fasteners next to appropriate pieces. If desired, tape them to the piece with masking tape. (Put the small pieces in sandwich bags; tape the bag to its

matching component.) Extra joining devices are sometimes included. Set these and any finishing pieces aside.

- Tape all pieces with masking tape and mark the name of the piece (top, bottom, sides) on the tape. This will reduce the time spent referring back to the diagram and avoids confusion between look-alike pieces.
- Check all predrilled holes to see that they are completely open. Bits of plastic or laminate often remain in the holes, making it hard to line them up later. If so, use your nail set to clear the hole.
- Read the assembly instructions completely before you start. Now you're ready!

Ready to Assemble (RTA) hardware

RTA (Ready to Assemble) furniture and shelves come with several common fastening devices, each with a specific purpose. Methods vary by manufacturer and item, but the most common are shown below.

Screws
They often look alike and may be similar in size, so sort them before you begin. When using screws on plastic or laminate, tap them gently with a rubber mallet to hold them straight while you're driving them in. Don't tighten them all the way until the entire unit is near completion. You may need to make adjustments or even swap screws before you're finished.

Pegs and dowels
Short wooden or metal pegs and dowels are used to hold pieces such as toe-kicks and top rails in place and may also be used when stacking units. Use a rubber mallet to tap the peg or dowel halfway into the hole (you can mark the halfway point before inserting the peg or dowel). Join the second piece and then tap it to hold the two parts together. Apply glue before tapping if specified by the manufacturer.

L-brackets
You may find them applied to toe-kicks or other small pieces, or to keep drawers square.

Shelf pins
The pegs of the pins fit into the predrilled holes on the inside of a piece so you can place shelves where desired. Each pin has a lip, on which the shelf sits. Use all four pins or the shelf will rock. Additional pins are available at home centers.

Cam bolts
These head-and-bolt combos are one of the simplest and most effective fasteners for storage pieces. Make sure the cam bolt is tapped or screwed completely in place or the joints will not fit tightly.

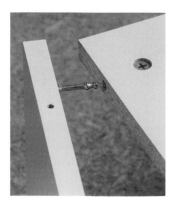

Cam-bolt savvy

Many storage pieces—from basic display shelves to box-style units—are held together with cams, a two-piece interlocking device. They're simple to use once you understand the mechanics behind them.

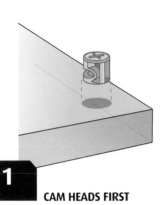

1 **CAM HEADS FIRST**
Insert the cam head into the predrilled hole. This hole will be on the flat side of the piece, close to the edge. There is a smaller hole on the edge in line with the cam head. Insert the cam head with the arrow pointing toward the hole on the edge of the panel. Install all the cams along one edge before proceeding to the next step.

2 **CAM BOLTS NEXT**
One end of the cam bolt goes into the adjoining piece, the other slips into the smaller hole on the edge of the first piece and extends to the cam head. Push all the cam bolts into one edge before going to the next step.

3 **TIGHTEN THINGS UP**
Tighten the cam head by turning it a half turn with a screwdriver. This locks the two pieces together.

WORK SMARTER

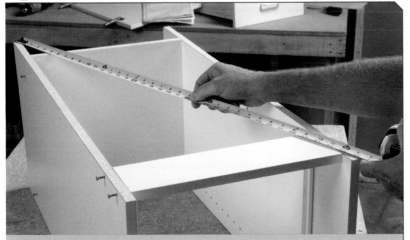

CHECK FOR SQUARE
To check if a shelving unit, closet starter, or cabinet is square before tightening the screws, measure the back from corner to corner in one direction. Now measure from corner to corner in the other direction. If the measurements are exactly the same, the cabinet is square. If not, tap it gently with a rubber mallet or simply manipulate it until it is square. Do not install the back or other final pieces until the unit is perfectly square.

SAFETY ALERT

BE SAFE, USE ANTI-TIP BRACKETS
Most larger storage units come with a pair of anti-tip brackets. If the item you purchase does not have them, purchase small L-brackets and screw the bracket first to the wall and then to the unit. Securing your cabinet or shelving unit this way keeps the piece from falling over if it is top- or front-heavy, or if children or pets climb on it. If desired, paint the L-brackets to match the cabinets and the wall so they are less noticeable. If the storage unit has a mounting rail at the back, or a back panel, it can be screwed directly to a stud and the L-brackets can be eliminated.

WORK SMARTER

THE LINEUP
If predrilled holes, tabs, or other joining pieces do not line up perfectly, maybe you've got the piece turned around or need to swap a piece for the opposing side. It's rare that pieces do not line up.

Installing wall shelves

Wall-mounted shelves and ledges are a terrific means of displaying collections—framed family photos, books, travel souvenirs, or china. Framed plates and photographs do best on shelves that have a groove or lip to keep them from slipping off the edge. Heavy collections will need shelves with support rails.

Display shelves are sold in three basic types:
- Free-hanging shelves appear to float on the wall; their attachments are covered by the shelf.
- Bracket-and-shelf sets are often enhanced with distinctively styled brackets.
- Track-mounted shelves have vertical slotted tracks attached to the wall, brackets that lock into the tracks, and shelves resting on the brackets. The tracks—often sold in white, black, and platinum—remain visible. You can accept that as part of the look or paint them.

Free-hanging shelf, with back plate

Mark the location of the shelf bracket, making the line exactly as long as the shelf. Place the backplate against the wall and mark the location of the fasteners. Remove the back plate, drill pilot holes, replace the backplate, and screw it to the wall. Slide the shelf into the backplate.

Free-hanging shelf, no backplate

1 **MARK THE SHELF-TOP LINE**
Making sure the shelf is level, mark the location of the top of the shelf on the wall—exactly as long as the shelf. Measure the spacing of the keyhole openings in the back of the shelf and transfer this measurement to the line on the wall.

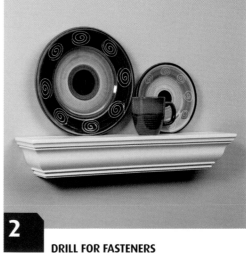

2 **DRILL FOR FASTENERS**
Following the directions on page 151, drill holes for anchors and screws or fasteners, depending on the fastening method required for the shelf. If the shelf has keyhole recesses in the back, leave the screw heads about 1/4 inch away from the wall. Insert the keyholes on the screw heads and pull the shelf down gently.

Track-mounted shelving

1 LEVEL ON TOP

Use your level and measuring tape to mark the location of the top fastener for each track. Follow manufacturer's guidelines for maximum spread between tracks.

2 PLUMB THE RAILS

Drill a pilot hole for the top fastener and attach the top of the track to the wall with a screw driven into the stud. Plumb the track with a level and mark the other holes. If you can drill the pilot holes through those in the track, do so. Otherwise take the track down or swing it to one side, drill the holes, and refasten it.

3 COUNT DOWN

When all the tracks are in place, count down the same number of slots on each track and mark that slot. This will keep your brackets on the same plane. Slip a bracket into the slots.

4 FINISHING UP

Hold each bracket about midway along its length and make sure both tabs at the foot of the bracket are in their slots. Tap the bracket in place.

5 LAY ON THE SHELVES

Lay the shelves on the brackets. Stand back and make sure they are level before placing items on the shelves.

Bracket-and-shelf display

1 ASSEMBLE THE SHELF

Assemble the shelf with the fasteners provided by the manufacturer, predrilling the holes if necessary. Hold the shelf against the wall and level it. Mark the location of the bracket holes on the wall and take the shelf down.

2 HANG THE SHELF

At each location on the wall, enlarge the marked point with a center punch and drill the wall so it will accept the fastener recommended by the manufacturer. Insert anchors if necessary. Thread the screws through the bracket holes and tighten them.

Installing track-mounted wire systems

Wire organizing systems are produced by a number of companies but share common features. They're composed of wire shelves, baskets, and supports that quickly screw together to boost storage capacity. You can purchase the components in packages designed for common needs, or individually to suit your own needs. Most stores will cut the materials to your specifications. Some items install directly into the wall with clips (see page 160–161); others install in slotted tracks and can be adjusted as the family's storage needs change. Installation for a track-mounted system is described here.

Adjustable shelf systems are exceptionally versatile. The shelf height can be adjusted in just seconds and you can install shelves of varying depths. Systems come with lots of accessories, from closet rods and hanging baskets to shoe racks. You'll always find wire shelving in snow white. Also look for steel gray and black.

1 PENCIL IN STUD LOCATIONS
Use a stud finder to locate one of the studs and mark its location on the wall. Measure from this mark to the next stud and use the stud finder to mark its center.

2 ATTACH THE HANG TRACK
This system uses a hang track screwed into wall studs parallel to the ceiling. Screw it into the top plate, the wall frame piece that runs the length of the wall and extends about 1½ inches below the ceiling. To start with, fasten the track with only the center screw.

3 LEVEL THE TRACK
Verify that the track can be leveled before driving the rest of the screws. If the track is right up against the ceiling and the ceiling is not level, the track nor the closet system will not be level. If so, drop the entire track ½ inch, fasten and level it, and drive the rest of the screws.

4 HANG SHELF STANDARDS
For most models, standards should be no more than 24 inches apart. Follow the manufacturer's instructions, aligning the standard with a stud, when possible. Hang each track plumb, using the manufacturer's recommended screws.

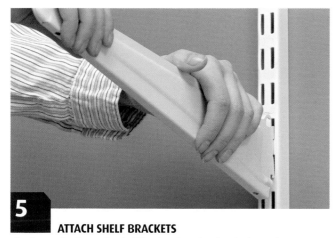

5 ATTACH SHELF BRACKETS

Slip the small tabs on the shelf brackets into the slots in the tracks. Press down until they snap in place.

6 CAP OFF THE ENDS

Place protective end caps on exposed metal ends of each shelf. Position shelves on shelf supports, making sure they rest firmly in place.

7 ROD SUPPORTS

Snap rod supports into the wire shelves, then drop in the bar to add free-sliding hanger space.

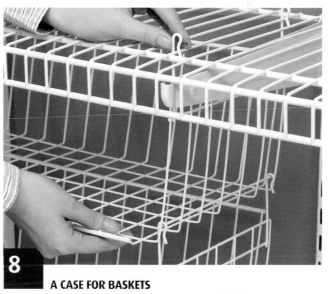

8 A CASE FOR BASKETS

Hang one or several baskets from the shelves to add shelf function where you want it.

 WORK SMARTER

GETTING THE PERFECT FIT

If your closet is too wide for one length of shelving but too short for the next smaller size, you have two solutions.

- Install shelves that don't reach across the entire closet.
- Purchase a longer shelf and have it cut to size. (Or cut it yourself with a hacksaw.) Round the length down to the next lower full inch. Have the wire shelf cut so that cut wires extend from the crosspiece far enough so that you can push on an end cap. End caps protect you and your things from cuts and snags.

Fastener facts

If your shelf standard will hang on drywall between studs, fasten with a drywall anchor or toggle bolt (see page 151). If your system will hang on a concrete or brick wall, install plastic anchors for the screws. Drill the anchor hole with a carbide-tipped bit.

Installing clip-mounted wire systems

I nstalling a clip-mounted closet system is a snap—literally. It doesn't take more than establishing the height of each shelf (which you can do by yourself or have done with the technology available at your home center), installing a few clips and shelf supports, and hanging the shelves. It's truly a weekend project.

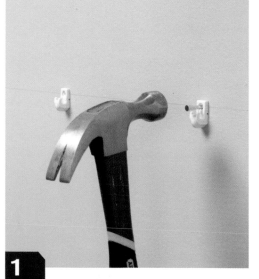

1

ON THE LEVEL
At each shelf location, scribe a level line with the help of a laser level or carpenter's level. Drill holes for anchors, if necessary, and attach the wall clips along the lines. Wall clips should be spaced no more than 12 inches apart, with the first and last clip placed two inches from the end of the shelf. Space the remainder of the clips evenly along the length of the shelf.

2

CUT AND RUN
If necessary, have your home center precut the shelves to proper length or cut them yourself with a hacksaw or jigsaw equipped with a metal cutting blade. File the rough-cut ends. Snap the shelves into the wall clips.

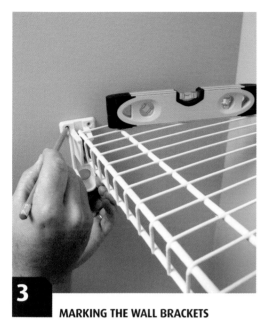

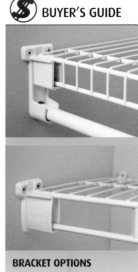

3 **MARKING THE WALL BRACKETS**

Cut the bracket template from the packaging if one is provided. Otherwise use a bracket. Pull up the shelf to approximately level (get help from a partner) and fine-tune it with a torpedo level, marking the position of the bracket holes. Drill the holes. Lift the shelf and screw the wall bracket in place. Snap the shelf into place.

4 **DIAGONAL BRACES**

At every other clip location, mark the wall for the installation of a diagonal brace. Hold the brace in place and mark the hole. Drill and fasten the brace according to the manufacturer's instructions. One brace is needed for every three feet of continuous shelving; a pair will be needed when installing a stack of narrow shelves.

BRACKET OPTIONS
There are two types of wall brackets for joining the shelving to the side wall. The bracket type depends on the shelving used. Both attach in the same way. See step #3.

Turning corners

There are two ways to wrap shelving around a corner. In new installations, using a continuous corner kit is simplest.

To add to existing shelving, two straight shelves are joined with a bracket.

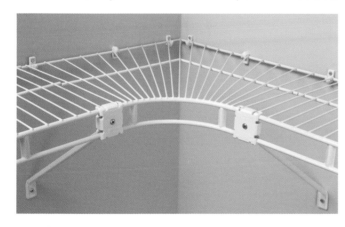

To install a corner shelf kit, mark the height of the corner so it will match the remaining shelving. Attach wall clips two inches from each corner shelf end and two inches out from either side of the wall corner. Snap the corner shelf in place. Add the remaining straight shelves and join them to the corner shelf with the joiner plates.

To join two straight shelves, measure so that the pieces will meet exactly. One shelf goes into the corner. The other butts up to the first. Cut the second piece so it fits perfectly to the first one. Both shelves install with wall clips; place the first clips two inches from each end. Add clips all along the shelves, spacing them evenly and placing them no farther than 12 inches apart. Add a corner support bracket where the two shelves meet. The flat bracket slips under the wires of one shelf and over the wires of the other shelf, giving the corner more strength and keeping the pieces level.

9

STORAGE PROJECTS

Installing melamine closet systems

PROJECT DETAILS

SKILLS: Measuring, marking, drilling, driving screws
PROJECT: Installing a melamine system

TIME TO COMPLETE

Installing an 8-foot closet system takes 4–8 hours depending on your skill level.

STUFF YOU'LL NEED

TOOLS: Pencil, tape measure, 2-foot level or laser level, electronic stud finder, screwdriver, center punch, hammer, power drill, drill bits, screwdriver bits
MATERIALS: Shelving system, shims

Solving closet clutter problems with a laminate system generally begins with a "closet starter." This is essentially a basic box that will be adapted to hold shelves, drawers, doors, or grids. Two starters are often stacked together to create a taller unit.

The starter unit can be augmented with a wire system as shown on the previous pages, or you can extend it with other melamine units whose construction is essentially the same as the starter unit. Here's how to assemble a starter kit with shelves and drawers.

1 **GETTING STARTED**
Clear enough flat space for all the pieces. Sort and label the pieces according to the tips on page 154. Set the drawer pieces aside. Lay one end panel on the floor and install the cam bolts (see page 155). Place the cam heads in the proper holes of the toe-kick, bottom shelf, mounting rail, and top. Slide each panel in place over the cam bolts and tighten the heads.

2 **ADDING THE OTHER SIDE**
Mount the cam bolts in the remaining side panel. Slip the panel in place opposite the first panel and tighten all the cam heads.

9

STORAGE PROJECTS

3 SHIMMING THE UNIT

If you haven't done so already, remove the baseboard so the unit will come flush against the wall. Use a stud finder to mark the location of the studs. Make the marks at about eye level so you can see them when you raise the cabinet. Place the starter unit against the wall. Using a carpenter's level, have a friend hold the unit in a plumb position. Drive shims under the legs to keep it plumb.

4 ATTACHING THE STARTER UNIT

Keeping the unit in the same position and holding the top snug against the wall, square the upper corner at the mounting rail with a framing square. Predrill the fastener holes in the mounting rail. Using a drill, drive a screw through the mounting rail and into the studs. Assemble the drawers according to the manufacturer's instructions, similar to assembling the starter or basic box.

5 RUN THE RUNNERS

Screw the drawer runners to the inside of the unit at the marked points. Slide the assembled drawers onto the drawer runners.

6 AN INSIDE JOB

Following the manufacturer's instructions, locate the position of the hanger rod brackets on both sides inside the cabinet. Attach the brackets with the recommended fasteners and slip the rod into the bracket. If the rod is too long, measure the distance between the side panels and cut the rod ³/₁₆ inch shorter.

7 THE OUTSIDE BAR

Locate and mark the position of the flange for an outside rod on the cabinet and install the flange. Measure the distance from the wall to the edge of the mounted flange and mark this distance on the opposite wall. Then insert the rod in the mounted and unmounted flanges and move the rod up and down with a level (taped to the rod, if necessary) to position the wall flange. Attach the wall flange with the recommended fasteners.

Adding pullout shelves

Roomy cabinets can be caverns— but you can tweak them to meet your needs, and without breaking your budget. Take a look at the projects on these pages. Do them yourself or ask your favorite handyperson to help.

Make a pullout shelf

If ready-to-install pullouts don't fit your cabinets or you'd like a different look, build your own. Finish them with stain and varnish or paint to complement or contrast. The basic box drawers here are made with 1× clear pine and cabinet grade birch or maple plywood. They're easy to assemble and easy to install with side-mounted drawer slides.

1

MEASURE THE CABINET/ASSEMBLE THE DRAWER
Remove any fixed shelves from the cabinet and measure the interior opening from side to side and front to back. Subtract whatever you need from these dimensions so that the completed pullout will clear the sides or rails of the cabinets. Purchase glides that you can mount without the necessity of adding spacing blocks behind them. Or mount spacers behind the glides so the drawer will clear the rails and door. This dimension is the dimension of your drawer bottom (adjusted for the glides). Cut the birch plywood to these dimensions. Cut the front, back, and sides as shown in the illustration (left). Assemble the front, back, and sides into a frame, with glue and finishing nails. Wipe off the excess glue and clamp the frame square until the glue dries. Then fasten the drawer bottom to the frame with glue and nails.

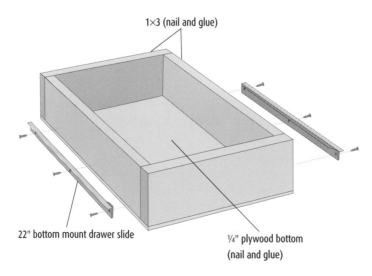

1×3 (nail and glue)

22" bottom mount drawer slide

¼" plywood bottom
(nail and glue)

2 ASSEMBLE THE DRAWER

As an alternative, use ¾-inch plywood for the bottom. Cut and assemble the sides and back and fasten the sides and back to the bottom as in step #1. Let this assembly dry. Then rip a 1×4 to a 3¼-inch width and cut it to the width of the drawer. Apply glue to the front of the drawer bottom and the front of the side pieces and fasten the front panel with nails. This will cover the end grain of the sides and the bottom and leave the top flush with the rest of the drawer.

3 INSTALL DRAWER GLIDES

Attach the drawer glides to the cabinet walls, installing spacers behind them if necessary to bring the glides in so the drawer clears the cabinet. Then attach the glides to the drawer box. Slip the drawer into cabinet glides and adjust them so it glides gently in and out.

 CLOSER LOOK

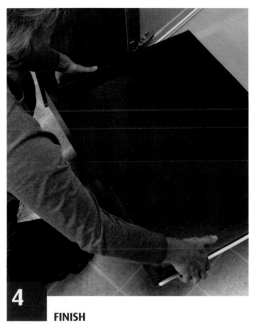

4 FINISH

Sand the drawers until surfaces are smooth and the edges slightly rounded. Finish with two coats of gloss paint or three coats of polyurethane.

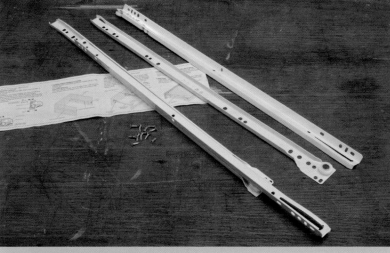

SIDE-MOUNTED DRAWER SLIDES

Prefabricated metal drawer slides take the guesswork out of installing drawers. One channel attaches to the side of the cabinet. A sliding bar fits inside the channel and attaches to the body of the drawer. The slides are sold in pairs in standard lengths and have weight-bearing guidelines. All hardware, templates (if any), and instructions are included, and there is room for adjustment after the slides are installed. Some slides are mounted on steel panels that become the sides of the drawer—so you need only supply the bottom, front, and back of the drawer.

Adding cabinet shelving

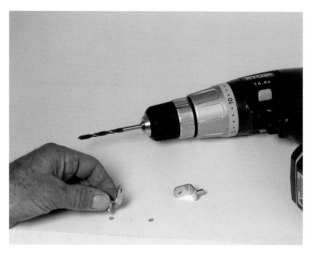

ADD HORIZONTAL SHELVES

If your cabinets are pre-drilled to hold shelf pins, just add shelves. Purchase shelf pins and have melamine cut to size at your home center.

MARK FOR VERTICAL DIVIDERS

For vertical storage, buy precut melamine dividers and hold them in place with shelf clips or other small right-angled metal clips.

ATTACH CLIPS

Mark the location of the rear clips, install them, set in the melamine divider, and attach the remaining clips.

CLEAT FOR STRENGTH

For a stronger installation, slip the melamine divider between cleats fastened to the top and bottom of the shelf. Precut the melamine divider so its finished edge will show.

ADD VERTICAL WIRE DIVIDERS

Many manufacturers sell vertical wire dividers in a variety of finishes. These kits fasten with clips to the rear, top, and bottom of the cabinet.

9

STORAGE PROJECTS

Tracking devices

Manufacturers now produce affordable, easy-to-install pullouts that will solve your recycling problems in a jiffy. Rolling recycling bins mount in your existing cabinets in less time than it takes to empty them. They're available in a variety of widths, colors, and configurations, from single-container units to two-, three-, and even four-bin racks. (This one comes with a washable heavy-duty cloth bag for paper trash). All of them come with a complete set of mounting hardware and most require only a screwdriver or cordless drill to complete the installation.

1

INSTALL THE TRACKS

Following the manufacturer's directions, either line up the tracks at the proper width or insert the pullout unit in the tracks and set the assembly in the cabinet opening. Square the tracks with the cabinet and mark the placement of the mounting holes. Remove the assembly and predrill the holes. Then fasten the tracks to the base of the cabinets with the proper screws. Tighten the screws moderately to allow for final adjustment.

BUYER'S GUIDE

THE MINIMUM OPENING

Measure the minimum opening of your cabinets before you purchase the pullout unit. The minimum opening will vary with the construction of the cabinet and the hinging of the doors. On frameless cabinets, open the doors fully and measure the distance between their back edges (it's often as much as ⅝ inch less than the cabinet width). On framed cabinets with externally hinged doors, measure the distance between the frames. If the doors are set inside the frame, measure the distance between the frames or the rear edges of the doors, whichever is narrower. Then measure the depth of the cabinet, and subtract from ½ inch to ¾ inch to allow for clearance when the door is closed. Purchase a pullout unit whose dimensions are less than your measurements.

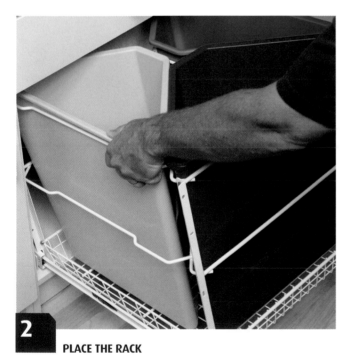

2

PLACE THE RACK

Insert the pullout unit in the tracks. Most designs require tipping the unit so its rear rollers slide between the front track rollers and lowering the unit as you push it to the rear of the cabinet. Slide the unit gently into place.

3

TEST THE TRACK AND TIGHTEN THE SCREWS

Slide the unit slowly in and out of the cabinet. It should move freely along the entire length of the track. Adjust the track if necessary by moving the track slightly to one side or the other. When the unit moves freely, tighten the screws securely.

9

STORAGE PROJECTS

Rolling out a wire rack

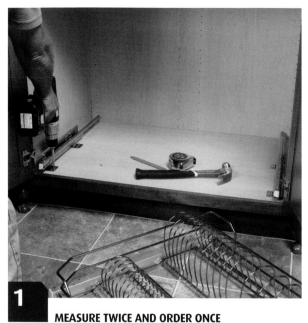

1 **MEASURE TWICE AND ORDER ONCE**

Although this kind of pullout wire tray is designed to fit almost every size cabinet, measure your cabinet twice so you can order the right size. Set all the parts out where you can get to them and fasten the bottom glides to the base and sides of the cabinet according to the manufacturer's directions.

2 **ESTABLISH THE TRAY**

Some cabinet models feature trays that slide in horizontally, others require entry from an angle. Insert the tray following the manufacturer's specifications. If the tray unit binds, don't force it. Pull it out and start again.

3 **LOAD IT UP**

Load up the dishes you intend to store on the tray and pull it in and out to make sure everything moves smoothly. If adjustments are necessary (the weight of the dishes may require this), make them now.

GOOD IDEA

TILT-OUTS

That space on the front of the base cabinet just under the front edge of the sink harbors more room than you might think. Put it to use with a tilt-out kit. It's a great place for dish brushes, scrubbing pads, and sponges.

9

STORAGE PROJECTS

Hidden but close at hand

■ There's no end to the storage you can find under a table—any table—from a 4×6 working surface in the hobby room, to a small round table you can pick up at the unfinished wood furniture store. The key to making them work is to find containers that will fit comfortably in their limited space. See-through plastic boxes with lids are good. Try shoeboxes—many of the shoe styles sold today come in boxes almost as hardy as the shoe itself. Have your child decorate one for a pencil

container in bright colors. That way it won't get easily lost. Leave the solution open to view or cover it up when company is coming. Attach skirting to the edge of the table. Overhang a rod pocket, grommeted, or curtain-clipped fabric skirt with a tension rod, a flat fabric panel with hook-and-eye tape, or cup hooks and loops. Choose a cover that doesn't impede access to your storage.

 **WORK SMARTER**

SMOOTH SLIDES

Hardware is not necessary for every pullout storage solution. Lightly loaded shelves slipped into metal or wood tracks will slide without sticking when you apply a little wax. Just use a rag to rub wax into the surfaces that make contact during the pullout. Reapply as necessary. The wax doesn't stain or discolor surfaces, and makes for easy gliding whether the track and shelf are metal, wood, or plastic.

Freestanding cabinets and shelves

Melamine is the plastic-coated hardboard that's part of many closet organizers, shelf stackers, and freestanding cabinets. You'll find it with doors, drawers, and dividers. Truly a shelf-of-all trades, its basic good looks and easy-clean surface makes it a storage solution in both utility and furnished rooms of the house. Quality varies, so check display models for things such as backs (Do they exist? Hardboard or cardboard?), drawer glides, good-quality hinges, and edges that are all finished.

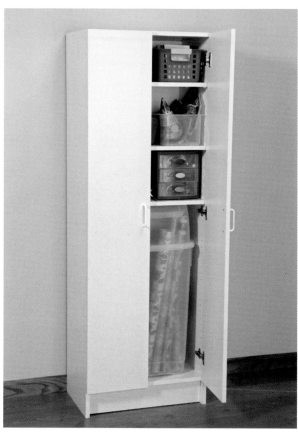

Assembling a melamine cabinet

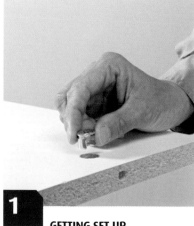

1 **GETTING SET UP**
Clear enough flat space to lay out all the pieces. Sort and label the pieces according to the tips on page 154. Insert cams in appropriate locations.

2 **INSERT CAM BOLTS**
Screw or tap the cam bolts into one of the side pieces. Be sure to install cam bolts in the top and bottom holes so the cabinet top and bottom are in the right places. Avoid placing cams where the hinges will fall.

3

TURN THE CAM HEADS

Slide one shelf (either top or bottom) over the cam bolts of the side panel and tighten the cam heads one at a time. Continue assembling the shelves to the side piece resting on the floor, tightening the cams on the bolts.

4

ASSEMBLE THE SECOND SIDE

With all the cam bolts and cams set in place, lift the side piece and set it in place. Tighten the cams against the bolts. You have now formed the basic structure for the shelving unit.

5

SQUARE IT UP

Place the cabinet on its front and measure diagonally from both sets of corners to see if it is square. If the diagonals are not equal, adjust the unit till it's square. Don't move it.

6

ATTACH THE BACK PANEL

Attach the back panel with screws and the toe-kick with L-brackets.

7

FASTEN THE UNIT TO THE WALL

Drill pilot holes in the upper rail, then stand the unit upright and attach it to the wall with screws or anti-tip brackets. If mounting screws or brackets are not included, use a 2½-inch #10 screw, driving it directly into a stud. Determine where to place the remaining adjustable shelves. Press shelf pins into the appropriate holes and set the shelves in place. Check them for level. Avoid placing shelves where the hinges will be attached.

8

HANG THE DOORS

Screw the hinges onto the door panels at the proper spots. Install the hinge plates on the inside of the cabinet sides so they align with the door hinges. Slip the hinges onto the hinge plates and tighten the mounting screws.

Assembling a wire shelf unit

Although almost all the freestanding wire shelf units end up doing essentially the same thing, they don't start out that way. You'll find a number of different assembly techniques. The one shown here is representative. Techniques and instructions differ by brand and complexity of the unit.

 WORK SMARTER

MAKE ASSEMBLY EASY
Apply dish liquid to parts that will join—rings and pole inserts—to lubricate them. The pieces fit tight and the lube will help you press them together with less effort.

1

ASSEMBLE THE PIECES
Clear enough flat space for all the pieces. Sort and label all the pieces according to the tips on page 154.

Starting at the bottom, slip an upright pole into each of the rings at the corner of the bottom shelf. Lock the pieces in place by pressing on them.

Continue building the unit from the bottom up, adding shelves and uprights as you work your way to the top. After the basic shelf is constructed, add any end caps or decorative pieces. This will vary with the style of shelf. See your package directions and photographs for details.

Assembling a plastic ventilated shelf set

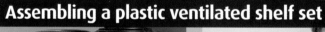

Starting with the bottom shelf, slip an upright pole into each of the rings at the corner of the bottom shelf. Lock the pieces in place by pressing on them. Continue building the shelf from the bottom up, adding shelves and uprights as you work your way to the top. After the basic shelf is constructed, add any end caps.

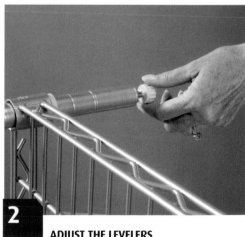

2

ADJUST THE LEVELERS
Tip the shelf to the back and adjust the levelers at the base of the legs by screwing or pulling them (however your particular brand works). If the shelf does not sit level, many have self-leveling legs. Adjust the leveling pieces so the shelf is stable. Use your level to make sure it is not tipped one way or another.

9

STORAGE PROJECTS

Assembling a metal shelving unit

Metal utility shelving units come in a variety of grades, some with all-metal shelves, and some with metal shelves into which a plywood reinforcement drops. What follows are instructions for assembling the metal-plus-plywood variety. Techniques and instructions vary by brand.

1 PREPARE THE AREA

Clear enough flat space for all the pieces. Sort and label all the pieces according to the tips on page 154.

Begin assembling the shelf from the bottom up by joining two uprights with one short side piece. Bolts on the shelf beams will slip into the keyholes of the uprights. Leave one slot open at the bottom of the uprights to form the legs. Repeat this procedure for the opposite side.

Join the side panels in the same manner using the front and back shelf beams. You now have the base of the unit constructed. Lay the plywood shelf in place.

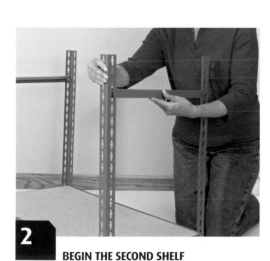

2 BEGIN THE SECOND SHELF

Add a second shelf in the same manner, constructing the form first and then adding the shelf.

3 MAKE THE SHELF TALLER

To make the shelf taller, add another set of uprights and more shelves. Join the uprights by fitting one shelf rivet into the bottom beam and the other into the top beam. Construct the shelf as before, lay the wood in place, and keep adding shelves until you have what you want.

Move the finished unit to its location, level it with shims, and attach it to the wall with the anti-tip tabs or by anchoring it through the keyholes. Use anchors appropriate for the backing wall.

Assembling plastic storage units

Plastic storage units haven't completely taken over the storage market yet, but their popularity is an indication of consumer response to a product that is relatively inexpensive, easy to assemble, requires little or no maintenance, and will last pr forever.

Because they're made from plastics (resins actually), their assembly doesn't resemble that of storage solutions built from other materials. Some models have parts that snap together throughout. Others rely on screws for some parts of the assembly (in combination, of course, with snap-together joints).

Because this material can be molded into endless shapes and configurations, you'll find vertical units, horizontal bins, extra-deep sheds, and small sheds with lids. The installation shown here represents one of the easier models to put together. Some require certain parts to be assembled with the unit on its back, front, or side. Most joints are made by sliding self-locking pieces together.

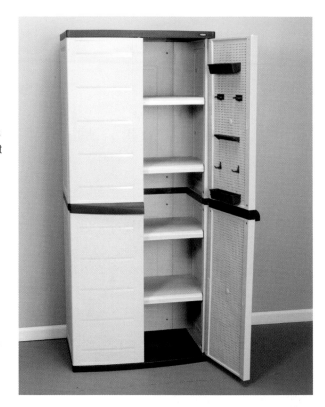

WORK SMARTER

DONE-IT-BEFORE TIP
Most shelving and storage cases are made of plastic that has a slight amount of give to it. The shelves often fit tightly and may appear to be too large for the frame. If the shelves don't easily pop into place, apply a little dish detergent to the joints. Slide the shelves in at an angle with the left side lower than the right side. Lock the left side in place, then lower the right side and lock it in place, bowing the sides of the cabinet slightly if needed. This will ensure that there is a good, tight fit. Do not bow the edges of rigid plastic pieces.

1

Prep steps
Clear a flat space approximately double the size of your finished piece. Large items often have to be flipped from side to side or front to back as you work on them, so be sure to allow plenty of room. Sort and label all the pieces according to the tips on page 154. Set the base plate on the floor and insert the lower back and side pieces.

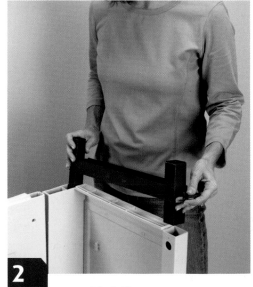

2

Insert side bridges
Find the black pieces that look like legs and push them into the recesses in one side panel. Repeat the process until the back panels and rear side panels are in place. Don't worry if the unit isn't perfectly square. You shore it up as additional pieces are added.

3 ASSEMBLE DOOR PANELS

Lock together the upper and lower panels that form one of the doors and fasten it to the side panels as directed by the manufacturer's instructions. In some cabinets the door pins snap into place after five sides of the shed are assembled.

4 INSTALL TOP PLATE

Set the top plate in place, with the corner extensions lined up with the recess in the side panels, and drive the top plate into the unit with a rubber mallet. You may find it easier to tap one corner a little at a time until you can seat each of the corners.

📖 WORK SMARTER

BEFORE YOU START

- Apply liquid dish detergent on dovetail and snap joints and vertical support joints before assembly. It acts as a lubricant and helps the pieces fit together more easily. The lube also helps if pieces have to be slipped apart to insert a forgotten piece. Spray lubricants can also be used, but they do not fill the joint spaces as well as detergent.

- To keep screws from going askew on plastic pieces, gently tap them in place with a rubber mallet to get them started. Once they are aligned in the hole, use a screwdriver or drill to drive them.

5 POSITION SHELVING

To set the shelving, first determine where you want it and insert the shelf into the unit at an angle. Raise one corner of the shelf above the shelf support that will put it at the correct height and push down slightly on this corner.

6 LOCK SHELVING

Lower the other end of the shelf until it comes in contact with the shelf support. Then push both sides of the shelf into place.

📖 WORK SMARTER

OUTDOOR SHEDS

If you are assembling a large outdoor shed, you'll need to take a few extra steps. The ground must be leveled, and any areas of fill should be tamped—pressed down—to prevent settling. Many large units come with anchors that can be driven through the floor and into the ground. Because the pieces are large, dovetail joints will need to be lubricated with liquid detergent and tapped with a rubber mallet to slide them together.

Building a window storage seat

 PROJECT DETAILS

SKILLS: Measuring and layout, using power tools, making butt joints

PROJECT: Building and installing a window seat with a concealed storage compartment

 TIME TO COMPLETE

EXPERIENCED: 2 days
HANDY: 3 days
NOVICE: 4 days

 STUFF YOU'LL NEED

TOOLS: Tablesaw, router, rabbeting bit, plate joiner, drill with drill bits and screwdriver bits, hammer, nail set, tape measure, combination square, straightedge, chisel, clamps, rubber mallet, hearing protection, safety glasses, dust mask, cotton swab

MATERIALS: ¾-inch birch plywood (BP), 1×6 trim, 2-inch and 1¼-inch drywall screws, ¾-inch brads, 6d nails, glue, ½-inch plywood, wood joiner biscuits, baseboard,

Window seats add grace and storage to a room. It's not something that works everywhere, nor is it something that you can go out and buy at the store. Each room is different, and if you want a window seat, you'll have to make one yourself, or have it made.

There are three distinct stages to building this window seat—building the box, building the frame-and-panel facade, and installing the unit.

Building the box is relatively easy, as it simply screws together. Given that the home center or hardware store will cut the pieces for you, and given that they'll do a better job than a lot of home craftsmen on a tablesaw, there's not a lot that can go wrong.

Building the facade is slightly more complicated, but the use of plate joiners keeps it from getting out of control. If you can make square cuts and handle large flat glue-ups, you'll do fine. The plate joiner handles what would otherwise be difficult joinery. It cuts a groove in each of the pieces to be joined. A football-shaped spline goes halfway into one groove. The groove in the other piece goes over the other half of the football. Assemble it with some glue, and you have a tight joint.

When you look at the steps involved in installation, it may seem complicated. In fact, the project consists of a lot of simple steps, most of which involve covering up plywood with solid wood or screwing a support piece to the underside of another piece of wood.

Materials chart

PART	FINISHED SIZE			MAT.	QTY.		PART	FINISHED SIZE			MAT.	QTY.
	T	W	L					T	W	L		
A lid	¾"	19⅜"	50"	BP	1		I front horizontal trim	¼"	1½"	48½"	pine	2
B hinge rail	¾"	2"	50"	BP	1		J side horizontal trim	¼"	1½"	19"	pine	2
C sides	¾"	16"	19"	BP	2		K side horizontal trim	¼"	1½"	16¼"	pine	2
D front	¾"	16"	48"	BP	1		L vertical trim	¼"	1½"	13"	pine	9
E back	¾"	16"	48"	BP	1		M angled trim	¼"	1½"	13¾"	pine	2
F upper supports	¾"	3½"	19"	BP	3		N bottom*	½"	17¾"	46½"	BP	1
G lower supports	¾"	3½"	16⅞"	BP	3		O bottom cleats*	¾"	3½"	23⅝"	BP	4
H cross support	1¼"	1½"	46½"	pine	1		* optional					

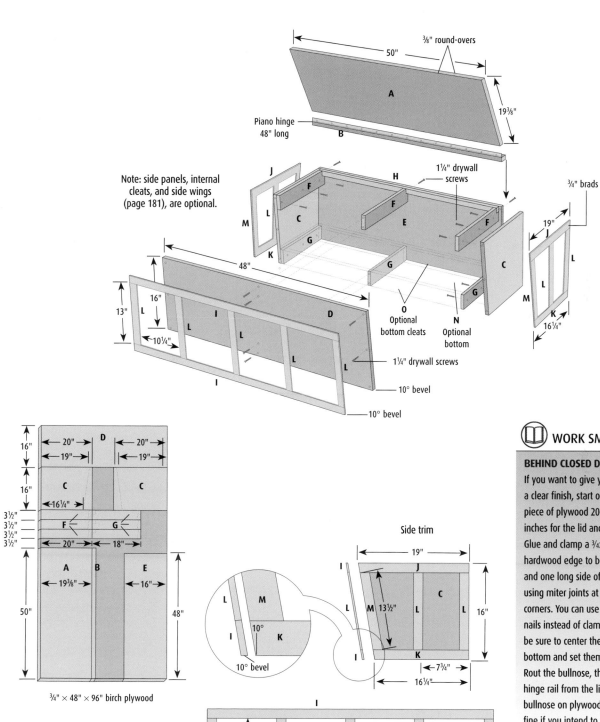

⅜" round-overs

50"

A

19⅜"

Piano hinge
48" long

B

Note: side panels, internal
cleats, and side wings
(page 181), are optional.

J

F

H

1¼" drywall
screws

¾" brads

M   L   C

F

E

F

19"   J

L

G

L

L

C

48"

G

M

K   C

16¼"

13"   16"

L

D

O   N

K

L   I   L   L

Optional
bottom cleats

Optional
bottom

10¼"

L

1¼" drywall screws

I

10° bevel

10° bevel

16"

20"   D   20"

16"   19"   19"

16"   C   C

16¼"

3½"   F   G
3½"
3½"
3½"   20"   18"

A   B   E

19⅜"   16"

50"   48"

¾" × 48" × 96" birch plywood

Side trim

19"

I   J

L   M   13½"   C   L   16"

I   L

10°   K

I   K

10° bevel   7¾"

16¼"

I

L   13"   L   L   L   L

11⅜"   I   11⅜"

23½"   23½"

1½"

Front trim

⬚ WORK SMARTER

BEHIND CLOSED DOORS
If you want to give your bench
a clear finish, start out with a
piece of plywood 20⅝×48½
inches for the lid and hinge rail.
Glue and clamp a ¾×¾-inch
hardwood edge to both ends
and one long side of the piece,
using miter joints at the front
corners. You can use 4d finishing
nails instead of clamps, but
be sure to center them top to
bottom and set them deeply.
Rout the bullnose, then rip the
hinge rail from the lid. Routing a
bullnose on plywood also works
fine if you intend to paint the
lid. Just fill the voids in the edge
of the plywood with wood putty
before you paint.

9

STORAGE PROJECTS

Making the box

1

ASSEMBLE THE SIDES

The heart of the window seat is a box made of ¾-inch birch plywood. Have the pieces cut to size when you buy your plywood. Start construction by screwing the front, back, and sides together with 2-inch drywall screws.

2

ATTACH THE BOTTOM

Draw a line ⅜ inch in from the edge all the way around the bottom. Put the bottom over the sides. Drive screws through the line into two corners along one of the ends. Go to the other end, and slide the plywood over so it closes any gaps and squares up the assembly. Screw through the lines at the corners. Drive screws every 8 to 12 inches along the lines on all four sides.

Cut the plywood at the home center

Wrestling big pieces of plywood across the tablesaw can be tricky, hard, and even dangerous. Lumberyards and home centers have special saws that simplify making accurate cuts. Draw up your plans, figure out how big the pieces need to be, and then have the store cut the parts to size for you. The pieces will be more accurate than any you could cut at home.

3

ATTACH THE FEET

Screw three or four strips of plywood to the bottom, spacing them equally along the length of the box. This lifts the bottom off any irregularities in the floor, helping to prevent the box from rocking.

4

PUT THE BOX IN PLACE

Slide the box into the opening by the window, pushing it against the back wall and centering it between the two side walls of the opening. Screw it to studs in the back wall with 2-inch drywall screws.

Making the facade

Use a crosscut jig

Whenever you have a job that requires cutting pieces so that they are perfectly square and all the exact same length, consider using a crosscut jig with a stop block. Cut one end of each piece first so that it's square, and then clamp a stop block to the fence. Position the stop block so that pieces butted against it will be cut to the desired length, and then tighten the clamp. Put the square end of the piece against the block, slide the jig forward to cut it, and then repeat.

1 CUT THE PIECES TO SIZE

The facade is made of a frame that looks a bit like a ladder, with plywood panels that fit between the rungs. The rungs of the ladder, called stiles, are 2¾ inches wide. The sides of the ladder, or rails, are two different widths. The top rail is 3 inches wide; the bottom is 5½ inches wide. Rip the pieces to width and then cut them to length.

The plate joiner

The joints in this facade are made with a plate joiner. A plate joiner cuts a groove in each of the pieces of wood to be joined together. When it comes time to assemble the joint, you put a football-shaped piece of compressed wood into one groove and fit the mating groove over it. The glue makes the compressed piece of wood, called a biscuit, expand for a nice, tight joint.

2 FIND THE CENTER OF THE STILES

Because the biscuit joint must be centered on the stiles, you need to find the center of each stile and mark it on each end of the stile. Set a combination square to the proper distance, hold it against the stile, and make a mark. Mark both sides of all pieces.

3 DRY FIT THE FRAME

Put the frame together without using glue. Equally spaced stiles make assembly easier down the road, so cut a spacer to position the stiles in the frame. Assemble the frame, clamping the stiles in place as you go. If necessary, trim the spacer or cut a new one, and reposition and reclamp the stiles.

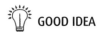 **GOOD IDEA**

NO STICK SOLUTION
The last thing you want is to glue the frame to the work surface. Cover the work surface with wax paper before you start to keep the two from bonding together.

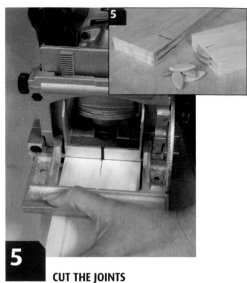

4 **TRANSFER THE LAYOUT LINES**
Use a straightedge to transfer the lines from the stiles to the rails. These lines mark the center of where each joint occurs on the rail.

5 **CUT THE JOINTS**
Set the plate joiner to cut a groove about ⅛ inch from the top of a stile. Align the line on the joiner with the line marking the center of the joint. Push the joiner forward to cut the groove. Turn the stile over and cut a second groove on the same piece, so that you get pieces that look like those in the inset. (See "The plate joiner" on page 179.)

6 **ASSEMBLE AND GLUE THE FRAME**
Put biscuits in each joint and put the frame together. Clamp the pieces in place, check for square, and fix any problems that occur. Squeeze glue into the grooves on one rail, and put biscuits into the grooves. Apply glue to the grooves in each stile, and slip them over the biscuits in the rail. The stiles can move back and forth on the rail, so align the pencil marks on the rail with those on the stiles to get the proper spacing. Repeat on the upper rail, then clamp the assembly together. Check to make sure the rails and stiles are square with each other, and make any necessary adjustments.

7 **ROUT AND INSTALL THE PANELS**
Rout the panels and square the corners with a chisel. Then cut the panels to size and apply glue to the inside of the routed edge. Put the panels in their openings. Tack the corners in place, and drive tacks every 12 inches along the sides of the panel to hold it in place while the glue dries.

Installing the window seat

1 ATTACH THE FRAME

Center the frame on the front of the box and clamp it. Screw it in place with 1¼-inch drywall screws.

Scribing the wings

Unless you are lucky, at least one of the sidewalls surrounding the seat is out of square. If so, you may have to scribe the side wings to fit.

2 ATTACH FILLERS AND SIDE WINGS

The assembled seat has lots of exposed plywood edges that you want to cover. Cut pieces to fit across the back, front, and sides of the plywood box. Glue and nail them in place. Then nail the side wings against the side wall. They will keep the lid, which fits between them, from getting close to the wall and scratching it. You can omit these pieces if you want the lid to extend clear to the wall.

3 ATTACH REAR SUPPORT AND HINGES

The lid needs a lip to rest on in the back. Cut a piece of 1× stock about 2 inches wide and screw it in place so that about 1 inch extends into the opening. Then cut the lid and test fit it. Screw a piano hinge to the lid. Put the lid in place and screw the hinge to the window seat.

🚫 **SAFETY ALERT**

SUPPORT THE LID

The lid for a window seat is large and heavy enough to hurt someone if it accidentally slams shut. Protect yourself—and others—from possible injury by installing a lid support. The support shown here automatically locks and holds the lid in place when you open it, and is easy to install. There are several other supports in the hardware aisle of your home center. Pick one that works best for the window seat you build.

4 APPLY BASEBOARDS

Apply baseboard across the front of the seat, mitering the ends. A short section of plywood is visible when the box is viewed from the side. Cover it with wood, and nail baseboard to the side. Nail quarter round to the baseboard.

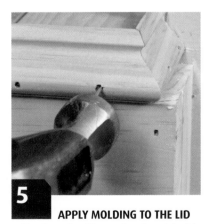

5 APPLY MOLDING TO THE LID

Nail a piece of molding to the edge of the lid and to the side wings. Choose a molding that is wider than ¾ inch, so that it can hold the cushions in place. Paint the seat, and cover the lid with cushions.

Constructing cubic storage units

9

STORAGE PROJECTS

PROJECT DETAILS

SKILLS: Measuring, cutting, gluing, assembly
PROJECT: Building and installing boxes

TIME TO COMPLETE

Nine to ten hours for a complete unit of this size.

STUFF YOU'LL NEED

TOOLS: Tape measure, hammer, nail set, combination square, 4-foot level, tablesaw or circular saw with rip guide, cordless drill, Forstner bit, counterbore bit, drill press, jigsaw, straightedge or chalk line.
MATERIALS: ¾-inch birch plywood (BP in materials chart), 2×4 lumber (CL in materials chart), European self closing hinges, shelf pins, drywall screws.

Modular makes things easy. Because all of the similar pieces are the same dimensions, cutting goes quickly. And because there are no tricky joints, so does assembly. You may spend a little more time making the first box than the others, but when one is done you'll pick up speed. You can't see it from the photograph, but you can from the illustration—the 2×4 base gives the unit some stability. You can also design and adapt these units for installation under the stairs.

The materials list includes what you need to build one cabinet with a door and a shelf. The instructions explain how to adapt the unit to your needs.

Materials chart

PART	FINISHED SIZE			MAT.	QTY.
	T	W	L		
A top and bottom	¾"	15¾"	23½"	BP	2
B sides	¾"	15¾"	28½"	BP	2
C back	¼"	23½"	30"	BP	1
D door	¾"	23¼"	29¾"	BP	1
E shelf	¾"	15⅝"	21⅞"	BP	1
F back supports	¾"	3½"	23½"	pine	3

PART	FINISHED SIZE			MAT.	QTY.
	T	W	L		
G base rails	1½"	3½"	to fit*	CL	**
H base crosspieces	1½"	3½"	10"	CL	**
I countertops	¾"	17½"	to fit*	BP	**
J toe-kick covers	¼"	3½"	to fit*	BP	**
K filler panels	¾"	to fit*	to fit*	BP	**

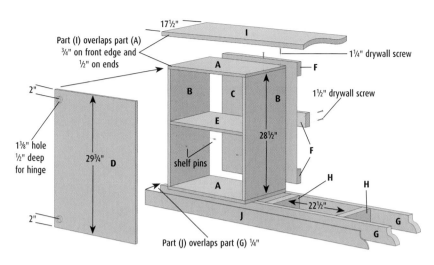

Part (I) overlaps part (A) ¾" on front edge and ½" on ends

17½"

I

1¼" drywall screw

A

F

2"

B

C

B

1½" drywall screw

1⅜" hole ½" deep for hinge

29¾"   D

E

28½"

F

shelf pins

A

2"

H

H

22½"

J

G

G

Part (J) overlaps part (G) ¼"

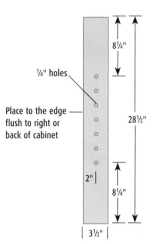

Shelf-pin drilling template

¼" holes

8¼"

Place to the edge flush to right or back of cabinet

28½"

2"

8¼"

3½"

Materials and finishing

The units shown here are built with birch plywood, edged with veneer banding tape and given a clear finish. Birch plywood also takes paint very well. You might also check the price of medium density overlay (MDO) plywood that has face veneers that are designed to be painted. Oak or cherry plywood with a clear finish is another option.

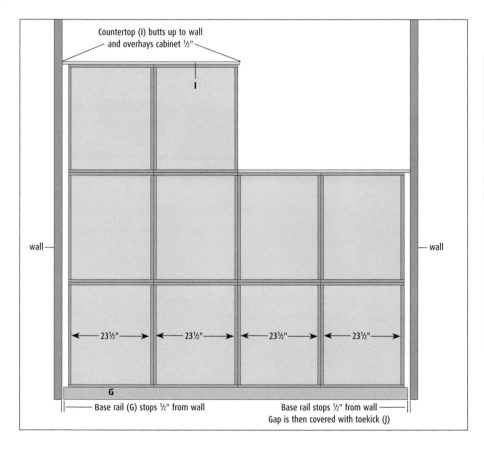

Countertop (I) butts up to wall and overhays cabinet ½"

I

wall

wall

23½"   23½"   23½"   23½"

G

Base rail (G) stops ½" from wall

Base rail stops ½" from wall

Gap is then covered with toekick (J)

9

STORAGE PROJECTS

Cutting the cabinet parts

1 **CUT THE STOCK**

To rip stock for the top and bottom (A) and the sides (B) of the cabinet, set the tablesaw's fence to rip 15¾ inches wide. Have a helper hold up the unsupported end of the plywood while you rip 15¾ inches from a full sheet. Or use a circular saw with a straightedge guide.

2 **CROSSCUT THE TOP AND BOTTOM**

Crosscut the 15¾-inch-wide piece into two pieces for the top and bottom (A) and two sides (B). If you will make a number of cabinets, you'll save time if you set up a stop block on the tablesaw.

3 **MAKE THE DOOR**

Rip and crosscut ¾-inch plywood to make the door (D). Then rip and crosscut ¼-inch plywood to make the back. Crosscut 1×4 stock to make three back supports (F). You can crosscut to a layout line with a circular saw or tablesaw or use a stop block on the tablesaw.

4 **DRILL THE SHELF PIN HOLES**

Make a template for drilling the shelf pins (see page 183) and set a stop on a ¼-inch drill bit to ⅞ inch so you'll drill ⅝-inch-deep holes. Clamp the template on a side piece, flush with the front and drill the holes. Then turn the template over, clamp it flush with the back of the side piece, and drill again.

Assembling the cabinets

1
ASSEMBLY LINE
First cut all the parts to dimension and put them aside for easy access. Grab the side piece and apply glue to the top edges. Put the top on the glued edges, flush with the sides, then drive 1¼-inch drywall screws. Attach the bottom piece the same way. Square the cabinet before the glue dries.

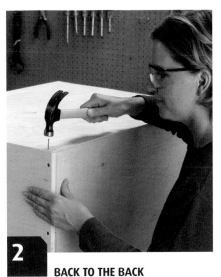

2
BACK TO THE BACK
Spread glue on the back edges of the cabinet, then fit the back to the side boards flush all around with the outside of the cabinet. Secure the back with 1-inch brads.

3
BACK SUPPORTS
Attach the back supports (F) with glue and 1½-inch screws into the back edges of the sides. Center one crosspiece and attach the others flush with the top and the bottom. If there is baseboard on the wall, position the bottom crosspiece so it will clear it.

Installing hardware

4
BANDING THE EDGES
Cover the front edge of the side pieces and shelves with iron-on edge-banding veneer. Cover all edges of the doors. Slightly round veneered edges with 120-grit sandpaper.

1
HINGING THE DOORS
To drill the holes for the self-closing hinges use a drill press with a 1⅜-inch-diameter Forstner bit. Bore holes 2 inches from the top and bottom of the door, ½ inch deep and 3⁄32 inch from the door edge. Check manufacturer's instructions.

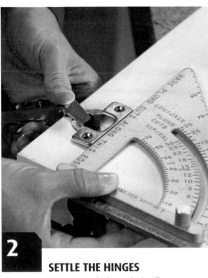

2
SETTLE THE HINGES
Place each hinge in its hole with the flange parallel to the inside edge. Mark and drill holes (usually 3⁄32 inch) for the hinge plate fasteners.

Installing the cabinets

1 **MAKING THE BASE**

Cut 2×4s for the base rails (G) to length. Cut enough base crosspieces (H) to place them 24 inches on center. Lay out the crosspiece spacing on the rails and assemble the base with 2½-inch drywall screws or 10d nails.

2 **MAKE THE TOE-KICK**

Rip ¼-inch plywood to 3½ inches wide and cut it to fit exactly between the walls. Attach these toe-kick covers (J) with 1-inch brads.

3 **FASTEN A CABINET**

Set the base in position and level it front to back and side to side, shimming it if necessary. Set in the lowest row of cabinets, predrill countersinks, then attach the cabinets to each other with two 1¼-inch drywall screws. Attach each cabinet to the base with two screws.

Installing filler panels

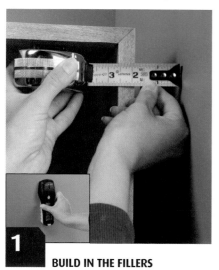

1 **BUILD IN THE FILLERS**

Find the studs behind the first row with a stud finder. Drive 3½-inch drywall screws through the back of the cabinets into each stud—just under the cabinet tops where they will be inconspicuous. The walls on either side of the cabinets may not be perfectly plumb, so the filler panels (K) may need to be tapered to fit. To find out, measure the distance from the top of the cabinet to the wall and from the bottom of the cabinet to the wall.

2 **CUTTING THE FILLERS TO FIT**

Snap a line between the points you marked on the ends of the filler panel. Cut along the line with a circular saw.

3 **CLEATING THE CABINETS**

Fasten plywood cleats to the front edge of the cubes and check the fit of your filler panels. Spread a bead of construction adhesive on the back of the panels and press them onto the cleats. Install the hinges and adjust them according to the manufacturer's instructions.

RESOURCES

The Home Depot continually looks for new products, materials and styles to help you with your home improvement projects. For the latest products available go to www.homedepot.com.

T=Top, C=Center, B=Bottom, L=Left, R=Right

American Woodmark
540-665-9100
www.woodmark-homedepot.com
service@woodmark.com
18TL, 60B, 73CL, 107B, 109T

BluDot Design and Manufacturing, Inc.
612-782-1844
www.bludot.com
44B, 96B, 102T, 102B

ClosetMaid
800-874-0008
www.ClosetMaid.com
3, 20, 21T, 35, 38T, 38B, 40L, 40R, 41L, 41R, 41B, 42TL, 42TR, 43TR, 43BL, 43BR, 46, 50T, 50B, 127TL, 127TR, 128T, 129R, 134, 139BR, 148

Do+Able
909-590-4444
www.doable.com
21B, 108B, 128BL, 136B, 139T, 142BL, 142BR, 143TL, 143B

KraftMaid Cabinetry
15535 South State Avenue
Middlefield, OH 44062
800-597-2202
www.kraftmaid.com
6-7, 15BC, 16TL, 16TR, 17TR, 18TR, 18BL, 22T, 24, 26T, 26B, 44T, 45TR, 47T, 61TR, 64TL, 70T, 70BL, 70BR, 71TL, 70TR, 70BR, 72TL, 72TR, 72BL, 72BR, 73CR, 74C, 75BR, 75T, 75B, 76BL, 77TR, 78TL, 79TL, 80CR, 80BL, 80BR, 81TL, 88TR, 89TR, 90-91, 93TR, 94B, 95T, 95B, 98, 100T, 100B, 101T, 103TL, 103TR, 106, 111T, 111B, 112L, 112R, 113L, 113R, 115T, 115B, 116TL, 116TR, 116B, 118, 119B, 121TL, 121TR, 121BR, 132B, 133B

L. Powell Company
800-622-4456
www.powellcompany.com
45TL, 45B, 48B, 49B, 51T, 51B

Mills Pride
Sold exclusively at The Home Depot®
800-441-0337
www.millspride.com
12, 14TL, 36, 37T, 37B, 39T, 39B, 42BL, 43TL, 49T, 56, 58BR, 60T, 72CR, 73TR, 74BL, 76TR, 80TL. 80CL, 97TR, 99T, 99B, 101B, 108T, 109B, 123B, 124-125, 129L, 132T, 137T

Rubbermaid
866-271-9249
www.rubbermaid.com
139BL, 140T, 140B, 141TL, 141TR, 141B, 142TR, 144, 145T, 145B, 146T, 146BR, 147T, 147B

The Stanley Works
1000 Stanley Drive
New Britain, CT 06053
1-800-STANLEY
www.stanleyworks.com
135B

Thomasville Cabinetry®
800-756-6497
www.thomasvillecabinetry.com
27B, 29T, 68-69, 73TL, 73BL, 73BR, 77TL, 81TR, 81BL, 84BR, 85TL, 85BL, 92, 93TL, 104-105, 110, 114, 117B, 126

RESOURCES

INDEX

A-B

Anchor, hollow wall, 151
Anti-tip brackets, 155
Appliances, storing, 74–75
Armoire, 27, 45, 46, 48, 99
Assembly essentials , 154–155
Back doors, 30–31
Baker's rack, 57
Basements, 40
Baskets
    bathroom, 58, 61
    bedroom, 37
    on bookcases, 97
    in children's rooms, 47
    in closet systems, 40, 41, 43
    hobby room, 121
    kitchen, 70, 83
    laundry room, 130, 132
    office, 117
    pullout, 17, 19, 70, 117, 121
    for visual interest, 18
    wire, 78
Bathroom, 52–67
    baker's rack, 57
    behind-the-door storage, 18, 60
    cleaning, 53, 62
    closet, 54
    developing style, 55
    functional display, 67
    kid-safe, 63
    laundry hamper, 66
    renovation plans, 54
    staying organized, 66
    storage layouts, 54–55
    toiletries and medicines, 62–65
    towels and linens, 56–61
Bed, storage under, 19, 45, 48
Bedrooms, 34–51
    children's, 46–51
    closets, 36–43
    furniture, 44–45
Belt storage, 43
Bench, 95, 176–181
Bins, 40, 146–147
Bookshelves and bookcases
    children's room, 48
    family room, 96, 97
    hobby room, 119
    tips for, 97
Bracket-and-shelf display, 157

Brackets
    anti-tip, 155
    decorative, 103
    L, 154, 155
Built-in storage, family room, 92–95
Bunk-bed frame, 51

C

Cabinet
    bathroom, 66
    built-in storage, 92–95
    corner displays, 85
    cubic storage units, 182–185
    fastening to wall, 171
    file, 112, 115
    garage, 134–137
    glass front/doors, 82, 83, 85, 101
    kitchen, 70–73, 76–81, 87–89
    laundry room, 128–129
    melamine, freestanding, 170–171
    office, 107, 108
    pantry, 78–81
    pullout shelves, adding, 164–168
    recycling bins in, 167
    shimming, 163
    sports equipment and household
           goods storage, 142–143
    square, checking for, 155
    top-hinged door, 77, 116
    upgrading, 17
    vertical storage, 71, 166
    wire rack, rollout, 168
Caddy
    for garden tools, 139
    for sports equipment, 140
Cams, 154–155
Cedar, for moth prevention, 41
Ceiling storage, garage, 141
Chest, bedroom storage, 45
Chest of drawers, 44, 47
Children's rooms, 46–51
    closet systems, 50
    color coordination, 51
    flexibility in storage, 46
    media stand, 49
    teens, 49
    tips for storage, 48
China hutch, 84
Cleaning supplies, storing kitchen, 86–89
Clip-mounted wire system, 160–161

Closet
    bathroom, 54
    bedroom, 36–43
    coat, 29
    design, 36–37
    front entry, 27
    laundry in, 128
    linen, 58, 61
    spacing in, 37
    utility, 89
    walk-in, 54
Closet system
    baskets and bins, 40–41, 43
    bedroom, 38–43
    children's rooms, 50
    choosing, 20, 38
    clip-mounted wire system, 160–161
    corners, 43, 161
    freestanding for mudrooms, 31
    melamine, 20, 162–163
    pants rack, 42
    shoe storage, 42
    track-mounted wire system, 158–159
    wire, 20, 38
    wood, 20, 39
Clothing, sorting, 10, 40
Clothing carousel, 127
Coat closet, 29
Color, 22, 51
Computer, 107, 110–112
Cork board, 117
Corners
    appliance garages in, 75
    closet system unit, 43
    kitchen, 73
    shelves, 161
Crafts center, laundry room, 131
Crosscut jig, 179
Cubbies, 14, 64, 94, 115
Cube, display, 83
Cubic storage units, 182–186

D

Design
    bathroom, 54, 67
    closet, 36–37
    kitchen, 75
Desk
    kitchen, 89
    office, 110–113
    rolltop, 115

Dishes, 76–77
Displays
    cubes, 83
    family room, 101–103
    kitchen, 82–85
Display shelf
    bracket-and-shelf display, 157
    free-hanging with back plate, 156
    free-hanging without back plate, 156
    kitchen, 82, 84, 85
    track-mounted, 157
Donations, 10–11
Drapery rod, 87
Drawers
    file, 112
    hobby room, 121
    home office, 112–113, 116
    kitchen, 71–73, 76, 88
    lining, 72
    pullout shelves, adding, 164–165
    touch-release, 73
Drawer slides, 165
Dresser, 44
Drilling, 152–153
Dry-cleaning, 40

E-F

Eating utensils, 72
Electronic gear, storing, 100
Entertainment centers, 98–100
Entries, 24–33
    back, 30–31
    front, 28–29
    mudrooms, 30–31
    stashes for small stuff, 27, 32–33
    strategies for, 26–27
Family room, 90–103
    built-in storage, 92–95
    displays, 101–103
    entertainment centers, 98–100
    freestanding units, 96–97
Fasteners, 150–151, 154–155
File cabinet, 112, 115
Food storage, 78–81
Foyers, 28–29
Front entries, 28–29
Furniture
    bathroom, 60–61
    bedroom, 44–45

G-H

Garage, 134–137
    cabinets, 134–137
    household goods storage, 141–143
    laundry solutions for, 87
    organization tips, 135
    pegboard, 137
    sports equipment storage, 140–141
    storage system, 21
    wire racks, 135, 136
    yard and garden tool storage, 138–139
Garage, appliance, 74–75
Garage sale, 11
Garden tool storage, 138–139
Glass doors, 82, 83, 85, 101
Glassware, 76–77
Hampers, laundry, 66, 133
Hangers, 40
Hardware
    anti-tip brackets, 155
    cams, 154–155
    choosing fasteners, 150
    drawer slides, 165
    hollow wall anchor, 151
    L-brackets, 154, 155
    piano hinge, 181
    ready to assemble (RTA), 154
    shelf pins, 154
    toggle bolt, 151
Hinges, 181, 185
Hobby room, 118–121
Hollow wall anchor, 151
Household goods, garage storage of, 141–143
Hutch, 60, 84, 97

I-L

Iron and ironing board, 131
Kitchen, 68–89
    appliances, 74–75
    corner treatments, 73
    design, 75
    desk, 89
    dishes and glassware, 76–77
    food storage, 78–81
    laundry solutions for, 87
    pots, pans, tools, and trays, 70–73
    shelving, 82–85
    storage system, 21
    towels and cleaning supplies, 86–89
Labels, 22

Laser level, 153
Laundry hamper, 66, 133
Laundry rack, 132, 133
Laundry room, 126–133
    cabinets, 128–129
    cleaning, 126, 130
    crafts center, 131
    iron and ironing board, 131
    pegboard, 130, 131
    raised washer and dryer, 127
    reach-in closet, 128
    surfaces, 130, 131
    trash can, 133
    utility hub, 130–131
    utility tub, 133
    wire systems, 126–128
Lazy Susan, 73, 78
L-brackets, 154, 155
Level mounting, of shelves, 152–153
Lid support, 181
Linen storage, 56–61
Lubricant, 172, 175

M-O

Media stand, mobile, 49
Medicine cabinet, 62, 64
Melamine closet system, 20, 162–163
Metal shelving unit, 173
Moths, 41
Mounting shelves, 152–153
Mudrooms, 30–31
Nail punch, 153
Nightstand, 44
Offices, 104–117
    desk organization, 110–113
    matching space to needs, 106–109
    paper records, 109
    staying organized, 114–117
Outdoor
    bins, 146–147
    sheds, 144–145, 175

P

Pantry, 19, 78–81
Pants rack, 42
Pegboard
    garage, 137
    hobby room, 120
    laundry room, 130, 131
Pegs and dowels, 48, 76, 154

Photo center, 48
Pie safe, 97
Plastic
    sheds and bins, 144–147
    shelf unit, 172
    storage units, 142, 174–175
Plate joiner, 179, 180
Pots and pans, 70–73
Professional help, 23
Projects, 148–186
Pullout shelves, 15, 70, 75–79, 113, 164–168

R
Racks
    bathroom, 57
    laundry, 132, 133
    pants, 42
Ready to assemble (RTA) hardware, 154
Records, storing paper, 109
Recycling storage
    bins, 167
    garage storage, 141
    home office, 114
    kitchen storage, 88
    in outdoor sheds/bins, 147
Renovation/retrofitting, 16–19

S
Sales, yard and garage, 10–11
Screws, 154
Secure storage, 19
Sheds, outdoor, 144–145, 175
Shelf pins, 154
Shelving
    adjustable, 46, 63
    back-of-door, 18
    bathroom, 63, 65, 67
    corner, 161
    decorative brackets, 103
    for displays, 101–103
    for entries and mudrooms, 33
    free-hanging, 103
    freestanding units, 96–97
    height, 14
    hinged, 77, 79
    hobby room, 119, 120
    kitchen, 82–85
    level mounting, 152–153
    pullout, 15, 70, 75–79, 113, 164–168

swing-out, 72, 73, 74
    ventilated, 38
    wood, 38
Shelving projects
    clip-mounted wire system, 160–161
    freestanding metal unit, 173
    freestanding wire unit, 172
    pullout shelves, adding, 164–168
    track-mounted wire system, 158–159
    wall shelf installation, 156–157
Shimming, 163
Shipping cases, 169
Shoe storage, 42
Shops, 122–123
Sorting, 8–9
Spice storage, 80
Sports equipment, garage storage of, 140–143
Square, checking for, 155
Stashes for small stuff, 27, 32–33
Storage
    making, 14–15
    principles, 12
    secure, 19
    types, 12–13
Storage seat, window, 176–181
Storage systems, 20–21. See also Closet systems
Studs, finding, 150

T
Table
    family room, 97
    hobby room, 118–121
    storage under, 19, 169
Tambour, 71, 74
Temporary storage, 23
Tension rod, 126
Tie storage, 43
Toe-kick, 185
Toggle bolt, 151
Toiletries, storage for, 62–65
Tools
    garage storage, 134–137
    for making storage, 15
    secure storage, 19
    yard and garden, 138–139
Towels
    kitchen, 86–88
    storage, 56–61
Toy-storage box, 48

Track-mounted shelving
    baskets, 159
    installing, 158
    wire system installation, 158–159
Track systems, for sports equipment, 141
Trash can, laundry room, 133
Tubs, for bedroom storage, 37

U-V
Undercabinet fittings, 16
Utility closet, 89
Utility hub, laundry room, 130–131
Utility shelving unit, metal, 173
Utility spaces, 124–147
    garage, 134–137
    household goods storage, 140–143
    laundry rooms, 126–133
    outdoor sheds and bins, 144–147
    sports equipment storage, 140–143
    yard and garden tool storage, 138–139
Vanity, 60
Veneer, 185
Ventilated shelving, 38

W-Y
Wall shelf, 156–157
Wet bar, 93
Window storage seat, 95, 176–181
Wire baskets, 41, 61, 78
Wire hangers, 40
Wire racks
    garage, 135, 136
    rollout, 168
    on wheels, 133
Wire shelf unit, 172
Wire systems, 20
    bedroom, 38
    clip-mounted, installing, 160–161
    laundry room, 128–129, 132–133
    track-mounted, installing, 158–159
Wood organizing systems, 20, 39
Wood shelving, 39
Workshop, 122–123
Yard sale, 10
Yard tool storage, 138–139

Toolbox essentials: nuts-and-bolts books for do-it-yourself success.

Save money, get great results, and take the guesswork out of home improvement projects with a growing library of step-by-step books from the experts at The Home Depot®.

Packed with lots of projects and practical tips, these books help you design, remodel, decorate, and repair your home or garden. Easy-to-follow, step-by-step instructions and colorful photographs ensure success. Projects even estimate time, skills, materials needed, and tools required.

**You can do it.
We can help.**

**Look for the books that help you say "I can do that!"
at The Home Depot®, www.meredithbooks.com,
or wherever quality books are sold.**